Education for a Pluralist Society

Education for a Pluralist Society

philosophical perspectives on the Swann Report

Graham Haydon (editor), John White, Malcolm Jones
Patricia White, T.H. McLaughlin, Stuart Devall

Foreword by Jagdish S. Gundara

Bedford Way Papers 30
Institute of Education, University of London
distributed by Turnaround Distribution Ltd

First published in 1987 by the Institute of Education, University of London,
20 Bedford Way, London WC1H 0AL.

Distributed by Turnaround Distribution Ltd., 27 Horsell Road,
London N5 1XL (telephone: 01-609 7836).

The opinions expressed in these papers are those of the authors and do not necessarily reflect those of the publisher.

ISBN   0   85473   263   2

British Library Cataloguing in Publication Data

Education for a pluralist society:
    philosophical perspectives on the Swann report. —
    (Bedford Way papers, ISSN 0261-0078; 30)
    1. Great Britain. *Committee of Inquiry into the Education of Children from Ethnic Minority Groups*. Education for all.   2. Children of minorities — Education — Great Britain
    I. Haydon, Graham   II. Series
    371.97'00941   C3736.G6G7/

    ISBN 0-85473-263-2

Printed in Great Britain by Reprographic Services
Institute of Education, University of London.
Typesetting by Joan Rose

159/11-001-005-1286

Contents

Foreword

Jagdish S. Gundara

The publication of the Report of the Committee of Inquiry into the Education of Children from Ethnic Minority Groups (Swann Report, 1985), presented to Parliament by the Secretary of State for Education in March 1985, has generated much interest and controversy. The Committee of Inquiry was initially established in March 1979 under the Chairmanship of Mr Anthony Rampton, OBE. It published its Interim Report, *West Indian Children in Our Schools*, in June 1981 (Rampton Report, 1981).

There has been considerable interest within the Institute of Education in the different stages of this Inquiry. Mr Rampton attended two conferences at the Institute pertaining to the Inquiry. The first was organized by the Centre for Multicultural Education in collaboration with the School of Oriental and African Studies, and it generated lively discussion amongst teachers, educationists and community representatives. The second, after the Interim Report had been published, was organized jointly by the Thomas Coram Research Unit and the Centre for Multicultural Education. Papers derived from this conference which were subsequently published by the Centre (Gundara et al., 1981), embodied major criticisms of the Rampton Report and highlighted such wider issues as the role of the state and education for equality.

In the second stage of the Committee of Inquiry, now chaired by Lord Swann, Professor Paul Hirst's teacher training panel visited the Institute and discussed issues arising from its work with many members of staff. Professor James Cornford, in charge of research for the Committee, also visited the Institute.

When the Swann Report was published, it again attracted considerable attention within the Institute. One outcome was the publication by the Centre for Multicultural Education of a critique of Chapter 7 of the Report (which dealt with language issues) written by Dr Verity Saifullah

Khan (Khan, 1985), Director of the Linguistic Minorities Project based at the Institute which had recently published its own research findings (Linguistic Minorities Project, 1983). Another was the series of seminars organized by the Centre in association with the Philosophy of Education Department, from which this Bedford Way Paper is derived.

The Centre was pleased to be associated with this stimulating series of seminars which was designed to examine issues raised by Swann in a philosophical perspective. The series attracted students, teachers, teacher trainers and members of the community at large. In now welcoming this publication the Centre would like to draw attention to the importance of such close analysis of official thinking on educational matters. The Philosophy of Education Department of the Institute has a long history of applying philosophical forms of analysis to the central questions of education.

Our thanks are due to Mal Leicester (Avon Local Education Authority), Phil Walkling (Birmingham Polytechnic) and Paul Zec (Christ Church College, Canterbury) who chaired the seminars and in their capacity as educational philosophers contributed to the discussions. Angela Hobsbaum of the Child Development and Educational Psychology Department and Kazim Khan of the Centre for Multicultural Education chaired the two remaining sessions. Graham Burchell, Teacher Fellow in the Centre, contributed a paper on 'Racial differentiation and justice in education' which will be published elsewhere.

The Swann Report has implications for teacher training institutions generally, and it is of paramount importance that the Department of Education and Science has a national policy which can ensure that the positive recommendations of the Report are implemented across the country.

Centre for Multicultural Education
Institute of Education, University of London
October, 1986

Preface

The chapters collected in this volume were conceived in 1985 as a discussion of the issues arising from the Swann Report, *Education for All: Report of the Committee of Inquiry into the Education of Children from Ethnic Minority Groups* (Swann Report, 1985). We did not intend to mount a comprehensive critique of the report; rather, seeing that the report brought up important issues which needed further discussion, we hoped to contribute something of value to that discussion from our point of view as philosophers of education. The issues themselves, of course, were already important and will continue to be important, independently of the fact that they are mooted in Swann. Hence, while each of these chapters takes its starting point from Swann, we offer them not just specifically as part of a debate on the report, but as contributions to the continuing debate to which Swann itself was a major contribution, on the way in which education should take account of and adapt to the plurality of cultures, ethnicities and faiths in our society. While some of the papers are critical of Swann, our primary concern is to be forward-looking, to make suggestions which are, we hope, of value in their own right. A knowledge of the Swann Report is, then, in no way a prerequisite to a reading of this volume.

Our general title *Education for a Pluralist Society*, seems to be that which best encapsulates the viewpoint which the chapters largely share; for all the contributors have proposals to make about how our society can best take seriously the task of educating for pluralism. It will be appropriate here to say a little about the notion of pluralism itself. It is a matter of fact that our society is a *plural* one in that it contains a plurality of cultures, ethnic groups and religions; but it is not similarly a matter of fact that it is, or will be, or should be, a *pluralist* society. For in some societies which contain a plurality of cultures and ethnic groups, one culture and one group dominates over the others. The form of such societies may be one of assimilation of minorities to the majority culture; or, avoiding euphemism, it may be one of sheer oppression. Neither can be described as pluralist, for pluralism, which is a matter both of institutions and of ethos, must at least involve some approximation to an equality of standing between different cultural, ethnic and religious groups.

Pluralism, then, is not so much a condition we are already in as something to be attained. It will be clear from the chapters which follow that there is a long way to go. But there are those to whom 'pluralism' does not denote something desirable. Critics of the idea include both some conservatives (who may favour assimilation) and, more interesting from the standpoint of this volume, some radical critics of current educational policy. Among the latter there is suspicion of the idea of pluralism, probably because it has often been linked in recent debate with the idea of a multicultural, as opposed to anti-racist, education. Multicultural education, which often consists only of bringing elements of different cultures into the curriculum and then sometimes only into its periphery, is seen by many of its critics as being at best too weak a response to the racism of our society, and at worst merely a strategy of containment by which the impression can be created that something is being done for minorities, while the institutional structures, both within the education system and more widely, through which racial inequality is perpetuated, remain unaffected. What is needed, it follows, is not multicultural education, which may only give people some knowledge of each other's cultural background, but a much more direct and combative anti-racist education.[1]

While the chapters in this volume do not explicitly take up the issue in this terminology, it will be clear that we do not identify pluralism with the status quo. Only where there is no domination of one sector of society over others, whether on account of customs, colour or religion — or class or gender — can there genuinely be pluralism. Any serious education for pluralism, then, must surely be both multicultural —for some understanding of the variety of lifestyles, beliefs and values in the society will still be part of it — and at the same time anti-racist. We hope that these papers will offer some pointers towards what could and should be done in an education which tries to be both.

To be more specific, the first three chapters, by John White, Graham Haydon and Malcolm Jones, all take up the issue of how differences in values and beliefs within a society can be lived with, without there being an out-and-out clash and conflict. The first two, taking their starting point from the view of Swann that in a pluralist society a common framework of values is necessary, explore how such a framework might be achieved. The chapters were written independently and it is best left to the reader to consider how far the approaches suggested are alternatives or how far they could be complementary. Malcolm Jones' chapter explores the notion of prejudice and suggests how, given an explicit awareness of the existence and nature of prejudice, an 'education for conversation' is possible.

Patricia White's chapter takes its cue from the vexed issues of self-esteem, or the often-alleged lack of it on the part of many black pupils. Whatever the truth about the self-esteem of pupils in our schools now, she would argue that the kind of relationships which will be necessary in a pluralist society will depend on self-esteem of a certain sort, and she considers what schools can do to enhance self-esteem in appropriate ways.

The final two chapters deal with issues concerning the nature of schools and of staffing policy in a society aspiring to pluralism. Terry McLaughlin argues that, within Swann's understanding of the underlying principles of 'Education for All' in a multi-faith society, there is still a strong case to be made for allowing the existence of single-faith schools of a certain sort. Stuart Devall, recognizing the extent to which institutional racism now stands in the way of pluralism, argues that there is a much stronger case than Swann recognizes for positive discrimination in the appointment of ethnic minority teachers.

Just as this volume is not intended as a comprehensive critique of Swann, still less is it intended to constitute a blueprint for action. For one thing, it should not be assumed that the contributors agree at all points. For instance, we would not all agree as to how strong a case there is for separate religious schools (a matter on which the Swann Committee was itself divided). But we would claim that each chapter has sketched a possibility or a line of argument that demands to be taken seriously in a society aspiring to pluralism. Comprehensiveness would be out of the question in a collection of this nature; and it was not part of the brief we set ourselves to tackle all the concrete questions of implementation which would come up in an attempt to put into practice the suggestions we have made. (Individually, though, we are developing some of our ideas and arguments further in other places.) What we hope as philosophers we are able to offer and have offered here are some critical reflections at the level of strategy and principle, which suggest pointers

as to the direction in which we think education should be moving if it is
to be an education for pluralism.

                              *   *   *

All the contributors to this collection are staff members, or present or
past students, of the Philosophy of Education Department of the
Institute of Education. John White, Patricia White and Graham Haydon
are reader, senior lecturer and lecturer respectively. Malcolm Jones
worked for his PhD in the Department; Terry McLaughlin and Stuart
Devall are, at the time of writing, completing theses on topics closely
related to their chapters in this volume. Stuart Devall and Malcolm
Jones are London teachers; Terry McLaughlin is a lecturer in the Education Department of the University of Cambridge.

    As Jagdish Gundara describes in his foreword, earlier versions of
these papers were read in a series of seminars at the Institute of Education in the summer of 1986, under the joint auspices of the Philosophy of
Education Department and the Centre for Multicultural Education. We
should like to thank Dr Gundara and other members of the Centre for
their advice and support; also Professor Bhiku Parekh of the University
of Hull, for his comments on five of the papers.

G.H.
October, 1986

Note
1. The issues touched on in this paragraph have been argued in many recent
   publications. For a variety of perspectives see, for instance, Craft, 1984;
   Troyna and Williams, 1986; Gundara, Jones and Kimberley, 1986; Hirst,
   P.Q., 1986.

The Quest for Common Values

John White

The Swann Report (1985) is historically of great importance. Its central idea is that all our children should be brought up

> to participate fully in shaping the society as a whole within a framework of commonly accepted values, practices and procedures, whilst also allowing and, where necessary, assisting the ethnic minority communities in maintaining their distinct ethnic identities within this common framework (ch.1. para.4).

The Report does not go into detail about what this 'common framework' of values might consist in. This seemed to me at first a defect, a failure to cash out a very abstract idea with all the rigour that this deserves. But I now see it as a strength. Spelling out what are to be our common values is an enormously difficult task. It is not at all clear that any small group of people, such as the Swann Committee, is the appropriate body to do this. The Committee went just as far as it legitimately could go, in urging us to think of 'education for all' as premised on a set of common values.

This may seem an unremarkable recommendation; but it is a milestone in official thinking about education in Britain this century. For the first quarter of that century the national education system was explicitly based on a dualist social ethic, which assumed different ways of life for the elite and for the masses. From the 1920s onwards the system was no longer officially constrained by any ethical guidelines determined at national level: schools and other educational institutions found themselves able in theory to set their own aims. In practice, however, they were constrained in many ways by central government policies; and the selective system flourished as vigorously in the 1926-1965 period as it had done before. Since 1975 the idea that schools should have this theoretical freedom has come increasingly under fire: professional control has given way to political control, the first tentative steps of Shirley Williams in 1977 having been followed today by the full-blooded centralism of Joseph and Baker. Logically one might have expected this movement towards the national determination of aims to be accompanied by, indeed based upon, well-articulated accounts of the wider ethical values on which aims must depend. But in all the flurry of DES, HMI and other official pronouncements on national curricula over the last decade, this has not happened. Between 1977 and 1981 what we had instead were brief lists of 'aims', jumbling together content-related objectives (like 'the effective use of language') and wider aims (like 'the development of lively, enquiring minds', or 'tolerance of other races and religions') without any attempt to sort out different orders of logical dependency or to articulate underlying value-structures. More recently we have witnessed Sir Keith Joseph's attempt to grab the education system by the scruff of its neck and reshape it to fit the demands of an ailing economy. This has involved plenty of central government directiveness at the level of curriculum content and examinations; and it has been based on a set of values which have favoured efficiency, individual initiative, competitiveness, industriousness, economic growth and consumerism, but put a low priority on critical reflection about the nature of society and its basic values, and on self-fulfilment through art, intimate personal relationships, civic attachments and self-understanding. Yet the favoured values have been taken as read: curricular prescriptions have been, and are being made on the basis of them, but there has been no attempt to weigh them in the balance with any alternatives.

The Swann Report marks a new stage in this historical progression towards basing the national education system on a common framework of values. The Joseph initiatives have followed through the logic of the shift from professional to political control as far as seeing that a coherent education system requires a coherent value-underpinning: Swann has moved on from this in not prejudging what the underlying values should be. The simple yet revolutionary message embedded in it is that the attention of the educational world must now be focused on working these out. It has brought us back, ten years late, to where the 'Great Debate' of the mid-seventies should have begun.

*   *   *

Why, if at all, is it important to establish a framework of *common* values?

Two kinds of reason seem to me cogent. First, members of ethnic minority communities living in Britain do not live and cannot live completely apart from other communities. They live under the same laws as everyone else, have the same political rights, are a part of the same economic system. Many of their aspirations and patterns of life are shared with members of the majority culture and other ethnic minority groups. This merging of outlooks, which often goes with eclecticism *vis-à-vis* the values of one's own minority community, is an increasingly marked feature of life in Britain today. Given these facts about our society, it would seem that any thorough-going value-separation between communities is out of the question. To that extent different value systems will have to be brought into greater co-ordination with each other.

Some critics of advanced industrial society will question whether a huge conglomeration of fifty or more millions of people like British society today can ever be sufficiently cohesive a unit in which to live a decent human life: they will argue that values can only be learned and lived up to within smaller-scale traditional communities. If so, then members of ethnic minority groups will do best not to turn to wider common values but should rather keep themselves very much to themselves. On the same analysis, members of the majority culture who happen, as most do, not to belong to religious or other traditional communities, can have no prospect of leading a worthwhile life but are doomed to a shapeless, rootless existence as part of the modern urban mass.

Critics of modernism like Alasdair MacIntyre (1981, pp.224-5) *may* be right in their claim that the new Dark Ages are already with us and that our salvation, like that of early Christian monks, lies within small traditional communities. But I cannot see how this can be *demonstrated*, at least at this historical time. For many people our amorphous society is not at all a bad place in which to live, even if they might wish it were not *quite* so amorphous. Like many others, I am not convinced that it is irredeemable. Indeed, I see the Swann proposals about common values as one way of making it more tolerable. This essay is addressed primarily to those who share this more optimistic assessment of modern society.

The second reason for looking to our common values is not necessarily connected, like the first, with the presence in Britain of ethnic minorities, although, as I shall show, it also applies to them. Much has been written in recent decades about 'identity crises' among modern youth (e.g. Erikson, 1968). One's sense of who one is is intimately bound up with the hierarchy of values by which one lives (cf. Taylor, 1985, Vol.1, chs. 1, 2, 4, 5; Vol.2, ch. 10). Since these values are drawn, often unconsciously, from the culture or cultures, including all kinds of sub-cultures, in which one has been brought up, any acute incoherence among these wider cultural values constitutes a threat to one's sense of one's identity. Our 'amorphous' urban society has been growing more heterogenous in its values for the two hundred years of its existence, not least for the last twenty or thirty, as more and more people have become disenchanted with the values of industrialism and what is left to us of Christian morality. Even if there were no ethnic minorities in Britain, there would be reason enough in the perplexity which people, especially young people, face in knowing how they should live — and their too-rigid espousal of some particular set of values which is often a reaction from this — to urge that we look more closely at our value inheritance and see if it can be better ordered.

For young people from ethnic minorities growing up in this wider, heterogenous society, their identity crises can be even more painful: they often have to contend not only with the Babel of values in the wider society, but also with the rift between that Babel and the traditional values of their own community.

*   *   *

I shall take it, then, that we have abundant reason to follow Swann's lead and attend to 'a framework of commonly accepted values' for our society as a whole.

How, then, is this framework to be arrived at? One way, it might be thought, would be to go by what values are held in common by all groups, including both the majority culture and ethnic minorities. But this would lead to a very *thin* common framework: it would include basic interpersonal values necessary to any minimally civilized society, like refraining (*ceteris paribus*, at least) from killing or injuring people, keeping one's promises and telling the truth; but very little beyond these. For instance autonomy, or self-directedness in the conduct of one's life, is highly valued in many circles; but since there are groups for whom it would be disvalued in favour of obedience to religious or other authorities, autonomy would not figure in the common framework. Once one moves away from basic interpersonal rules, which can be seen largely as injunctions about what *not* to do, towards more positive delineations of human well-being, there are so many competing pictures — some stressing hierarchy, others equality, some hedonism, others ascetism, some religiously-based, others secular, and so on — that there is likely to be little that all groups would accept.

There are places in Swann where it might be read as supporting just such an HCF approach to the identification of common values. But I cannot believe this is really what is intended, since among its occasional references to recommended common values one finds values which would *not* be favoured by every social group. Most prominent among these is its rejection of racism. On the HCF approach, given the existence of racist groups in our society, anti-racism could not find a place among our common values.

If Swann is not advocating an HCF approach, it must be pointing in the direction of working out what our common values *should be*, even if they conflict with the actual values of any particular group. (Indeed in ch.1, para.4, it states that 'ethnic minority communities cannot in practice preserve all elements of their cultures and lifestyles unchanged ... indeed if they were to do so it would in many cases be impossible for them to take on the shared values of the larger pluralist society').

How are we to go about this constructive task of determining our framework of common values? It was not Swann's job to tell us, but now that it has pointed us in this direction, answers to this question must be found.

A first step — long before one can proceed to identify the common values — would be to gain as much clarity as possible about what sort of enterprise it would be to determine the framework. How far would it be a matter of value creation *ex nihilo*? How far could it be forwarded by empirical investigation of values which are actually favoured?

We have, I think, to steer between two extremes. One is the utopian project of someone's dreaming up from somewhere a set of values without any prior consideration of whether the inhabitants of contemporary Britain can live by them. The other extreme is to take too much from the value status quo, i.e. to be too imprisoned by actual values. What I have called the HCF approach falls foul of this.

Steering between these extremes implies *both* getting as much insight as possible into actual values *and* realizing that such an investigation will not take us all the way, since in the end ethical judgements will have to be made about which values should be favoured over others, which values weighed more heavily, and which less.

Shall we need to import any values into our value-framework from outside those which our society actually espouses? I do not mean to be dogmatically negative about this, but we should remember — as I implied above — just how rich that society is in its value-orientations. It is heir to the value-legacies of numerous civilizations and historical stages in the development of those civilizations. Its ethnic minority communities have brought with them the values of Islam, Hinduism, Judaism, of modern Greek, Caribbean and many other ways of life. Its 'majority culture' is itself heterogenous, incorporating, among other things, Christian values of widely differing sorts, the atomistic individualism of the seventeenth century and beyond, the humanist rationalism and utilitarianism of the Enlightment, varieties of Romantic reaction against Enlightment values, civic humanism originating with the ancient Greeks, and the consumerism, efficiency and other values associated with an advanced industrial economy. It is doubtful, to say the least, whether we need look beyond the mass of values already in our midst to find what we need for our common framework.

The task of constructing this framework is perhaps best conceived as a 'sorting-through' of all these various values. Although none of the following jobs is independent of the others and, still less, assignable without remainder to a particular discipline like history, psychology, sociology or philosophy, this 'sorting out' involves:

1. Identifying the main value-orientations in the society, including covert, taken-for-granted, values;

2. Seeking to understand these values in historical perspective: seeing how they arose, how residues of older values have persisted, perhaps in a modified form;

3. Examining the logical similarities between apparently diverse values and separating out logically different values which have become conflated together;

4. Digging back to the fundamental assumptions and presuppositions on which different value-positions rest, including metaphysical assumptions about such things as human nature and the cosmos;

5. Examining the cogency of the grounds given for different value-positions, trying to penetrate beneath conscious or unconscious forms of rationalization or mystification;

6. Charting the unintended consequences of mass adherence to a particular set of values. By now well-known points about the 'social consequences of economic growth' provide one example here: not everyone who favours values associated with industrialism, like efficiency and individual initiative, is equally enthusiastic about the manipulation of the consumer to buy unneeded goods, or about crowded roads and pollution.

Recent work in ethics and social theory is helpful in a number of these directions. Jurgen Habermas's (1976, pp.xviff., 111ff.) work on the 'ideal speech situation' with its attendant ideas of one's understanding the origins of one's beliefs and one's being maximally free from the disturbing effects of others and other forms of ideological domination over one; Alasdair MacIntyre's (1981) analysis of our 'emotivist' western culture and its historical origins; Charles Taylor's work (1985), not least his paper 'Legitimation crisis?' (op.cit. Vol.2, pp.248ff.), in which he shows how over recent centuries two very different ideals of 'living according to nature' have become entwined together to form the basis of 'the modern identity': these are some examples among many of work which could aid us in the task of collective self-understanding about our values. This kind of philosophical-sociological-historical work, largely on majority values, needs to be supplemented both by more specific studies of *British* majority values (e.g. Martin Wiener's (1981) work on our anti-industrial, pro-rural predilections), and by similar investigations into ethnic minority values. Others will know the relevant literature here better than I.

*   *   *

In what way might a 'framework of common values' emerge from the enquiries suggested above?

It would be misguided, I think, to intend those enquiries to lead to a sieving-away of those values which are unsuitable for inclusion in the common framework from those which will constitute it. A common framework of values could be nothing like a national code. Who would decide what was left in the sieve? For one thing, how acceptable values are going to be is highly controversial; for another, disputes among values revolve less often around the black-and-white issue about whether x is in or out than around what weighting x is to be given *vis-à-vis* y or z. It is hard to see how the sieving model could function. Certainly if anyone thought that way, elitism and the authoritarian repression of nonconformists would be difficult to avoid.

The way forward, in my view, is to see the formulation of the value-framework not as a discrete, if revisable, act, but as an on-going and unending collective activity of society as a whole. It is hard for me to characterize quite what I have in mind, but it would consist basically in discussion, discussion directed to the question: what should be our common values? At its more academic end this discussion could follow up in a systematic way the sorts of tasks outlined in 1. to 6. above. But there is every reason, if elitist pressures are to be minimized, why as many people as possible should engage in it. To a large extent, of course, this already occurs — in ordinary conversation, in discussion of social events on radio, TV and in the press, as well as in more formal debates and pronouncements of politicians and others. But these more everyday discussions are often insufficiently reflective and informed, and the views of those in search of enlightenment are often difficult to hear above those already convinced that they have the answers — those adherents of some monistic faith, whether industrialism, Marxism, racism, dogmatic religion, egoism, the cult of machismo, flat egalitarianism, libertarianism, or whatever. There is no sharp line, of course, between 'academic' and 'everyday' thinking about values; and it would be good if the more rigorous and broader-horizoned work towards the academic end of the continuum could be brought to bear on our more ordinary reflections.

This many-levelled discussion could be characterized as both a collective and a personal quest for self-understanding. The latter I have already touched on in my remarks about the dependence of one's sense of one's own identity on the often hidden value structure of one's community. At the individual level informed reflection on values could help people to avoid or cope with and overcome the crises of identity of which I earlier spoke. But the quest for self-understanding can also be interpreted more globally, as an enterprise in some sense of our society as a whole. It is this collective interpretation on which one would rely in trying to elaborate Swann's basic idea about a common framework of values.

In what way, even so, would this many-levelled discussion eventuate in a *common* framework? Couldn't different individuals and groups, including ethnic minority groups, still end up holding very different values, however well-informed and skilled in argument about values they had become?

A certain amount of diversity would be both to be expected and desirable. Even if everyone agreed exactly on what things they valued and disvalued, there would be bound to be differences in the *weight* which different people put on different values; and attempts to reduce these differences — e.g. to make aesthetic values become of such-and-such a degree of importance in everyone's personal value-scheme — would seem to involve the domination of some people by others. Leaving aside differences in weighting, there would also surely be individual and group differences among values espoused or rejected: again, these would seem to be ineradicable except by indoctrination or other forms of domination.

Along with diversity one might also expect to see an increasing convergence in values. This would be likely to happen in three related ways. First, individuals and groups would be increasingly able, ideally, to locate their own value-hierarchies within the common value-stock about which I have been writing. They would see that whatever differences they had with others were only fully intelligible within wider value-horizons which were the common property of the whole community.

Secondly, and emerging out of this, people could be expected to become more accommodating towards those with whom they differed. Ralf Dahrendorf (1982) has recently referred to the polarization of attitudes that is now a feature of British life, in industry, politics and relations between social groups. As people become more self-conscious about their values, they also become better placed to see others not as with them or against them in any simplistic way, but as weighting shared values differently and as sharing a common value-stock in which there is much overlapping between different people's value-schemes even if items which are positively valued by some are disvalued by others. This way lies the possibility of compromise, of the peaceful and rational resolution of differences. If we follow it, those tendencies in our society towards intransigence, towards the conviction that only we, or our group, or our leaders, know for certain what is good or bad, right or wrong, will surely diminish.

Thirdly, as discussion of values gets under way, one might expect that some values which hitherto had been held unreflectively would drop away or become less salient as people found that they could no longer live by them. The intellectual activities 1. to 6. above, as they percolated through into more everyday thinking (in something of the way that geological and biological thought in the age of Darwin affected popular views of human beings and their place in the cosmos), would give more and more people something of the critical equipment they would need to think through received values, to question their grounds and the consequences of holding them. This, too, might well lead to greater convergence in beliefs: as happened with Darwin, I would hypothesize a further decline among religiously-based values; and I suspect that more and more people would question the weight currently placed on the virtues of economic growth, once its social and ecological consequences became more fully apparent to them. Positively, I would expect to see a convergence on those values — like friendship, family life, sexual love, co-operative social activities and expressive activities of artistic and other kinds —which lie closest to our common human nature as social, symbol-using animals conscious of our mortality. (More would, of course, need to be said — elsewhere — in support of this kind of argument.)

*   *   *

So much, then, for how the common framework of values might in general be conceived. Questions also arise about the institutional means by which one can move towards realizing this conception. As I have implied more than once, academics will not have a privileged role in the formulation of the framework or in the discussion out of which it emerges. But understanding and evaluating the actual values found in our society is a complex task, as we have seen, which draws on historical, sociological, psychological and philosophical expertise. Academics in these and related areas, including schoolteachers as well as university teachers, can help not only their pupils and colleagues, but people more generally to gain a deeper insight into the nature, the strength, and the weaknesses of our several values. Rather than withdrawing funds from work in this area and diverting them to science and technology, our political authorities could have placed, and perhaps will place, a high priority on value-studies, supporting them financially and in other ways.

If only the will is there, ways could also be found, I am sure, of promoting the quest for common values in non-academic institutions: in industry, in the media, in politics. Current moves towards worker-participation in industry, where not manipulatory, can help here, as can also the weakening of confrontatory two-party politics in central and local government. Television directors could spend less time on presenting superficial polarized discussions and more on deeper investigations, directly inspired by the collective quest.

*   *   *

How would this kind of 'Great Discussion' (very different from the 'Great Debate' of 1975 and 1976) affect, first, the 'education for all' that Swann envisages and, secondly, the ethnic minority communities? Since the aim is not a finally-formulated code of values, one would be able neither to base the aims of educational institutions on such a code, nor to rule in certain ethnic minority values as compatible with the code and rule out others as incompatible.

Taking schools first, one might expect their aims and curricula to reflect in time the emerging consensus on values, shifting as it shifted. In this way schools would become, as they should be, accountable to the political democracy in which they were placed — although just how this emerging consensus would be reflected at the level of central and local government would require more investigation. All this is very much in the longer term, of course, but, even at the beginning of the 'Great Discussion', there would be one clear aim that schools would have to follow, namely to begin to induct pupils into the collective quest itself and to develop in them the understanding, skills of argument and interpersonal attitudes necessary to engage in it. This reflectiveness, which one would expect to see more fully developed in older pupils, would have to go hand in hand, of course, with the more immediate aim of revealing to pupils, and not in any mere external way, a whole range of values by which they might live and on which they might come to reflect. I do not underestimate the ethical difficulties which this would place on those responsible for the content of education in our schools in trying to bring children up within a defensible and coherent scheme of values at a time when there has been so little communal reflection on such values.

Once again, how schools' aims in general and the more specific, reflective aim just mentioned might be cashed out in curricula and forms of organization is an important question, but one beyond my present brief.

The values of the ethnic minority communities can, except in one area, be left to flourish or wither as the reflective judgements of their members determine. Values unquestioned in a less open society but hard to accept once one has been exposed to a tradition of social critique might be expected to decline in influence; others — those, perhaps, which stress our sociality — may become more solidly entrenched as they are echoed in the common framework. No adult members of ethnic minority communities need be obliged to relinquish their local values, however out of step they may have become with the national consensus, and given J.S. Mill's qualification that they bring no harm to others.

The one area in which the larger community may sometimes have to interfere with local values is in the upbringing of children. Since the quest is one in which not an elite but the whole population can engage, children must be brought up in such a way as to enable them freely to participate in it. This sets limits to how far they can be brought up to believe that the values of their community are the only ones they should follow.

*   *   *

One final remark. I realize that a number of points in this chapter, not least those in the last paragraph, will be unacceptable to some people from ethnic minority communities — as well as others from religious or other communities within the majority culture. Not everyone will accept in full the reasons given near the beginning for moving towards a common value framework, together with the need for compromise in the search for mutually agreed solutions that this brings with it. Some *will* want high walls around their community, taking from outside only those values which fit in with it. To what extent this stance is rationally defensible is a further question. And if it *can* be shown to be defensible as far as *adults'* preferences are concerned, further arguments are necessary to show why adults are justified in trying to impose their own values on children. It is not self-evident that they are so justified.

Towards 'a Framework of Commonly Accepted Values'

Graham Haydon

The first chapter of the Swann Report outlines the Committee's view 'of the kind of multi-racial society for which we believe the education system should be preparing all youngsters'.[1] Rejecting assimilation and separatism, it advocates a democratic pluralism, in which diversity will exist 'within a framework of commonly accepted values, practices and procedures'.[2] As John White points out above, it does not say whether this framework is something we already have, or something that needs to be created. Education cannot initiate people into an existing framework if, as I think is the case, we do not have one. But if the framework is to be created, we do not have agreement on what its constituents should be. How, then, is education to prepare people for living within a framework of commonly accepted values?[3] It is this question to which I shall suggest an answer.

The sense in which I think we do not now have such a framework is that we do not have common agreement on values at a workably concrete level. A framework has to do something: it should protect people in some sorts of divergence from the norms of others; it should be determinate enough also to rule out some sorts of practice (or it would not be functioning as a framework of values at all); and it should provide some guidance in settling particular disputes within the scope of the framework. Clearly agreement at the level of lip-service to open-ended slogans will not be effective. Yet I think this may be the most that we have on the values to which the Committee refers: 'a shared commitment to certain essential freedoms and to fundamental values such as a belief in justice and equality';[4] 'an obligation to abide by the current laws of the country and to seek to change them only through peaceful and democratic means';[5] and various equal rights and freedoms which the government should ensure.[6] Any appearance of consensus on these values is liable to break down when they have to be interpreted in practice. On

25

essential freedoms, consider the differences in our society over freedom of expression, or over 'the right to work' in recent industrial disputes. As regards an obligation to abide by the current laws, quite apart from the fact that there is not a universal consensus against illegal violence, there is a respected tradition of civil disobedience as, precisely, a peaceful *and democratic* way of seeking to change laws, especially where those laws are themselves seen as undemocratic.[7] Diverse conceptions of what, in the way of distribution and redistribution of resources, would constitute social justice, are a major source of political disagreement[8]; while the commitment of some to what others disparagingly describe as 'the race relations industry' is just one illustration of the fact that, on various matters of equal rights and opportunities, any approximation to universal consensus can hardly, at present, go beyond lip-service to slogans.

*   *   *

If education has to prepare people for life within a framework to which as yet we have no more than an open-ended approximation, then, roughly speaking, there are two alternatives (with intermediate possibilities): either a decision has first to be made on what the constitutents of the framework are to be, before people can be educated into it; or the details of the framework will in some way be determined through the educational process itself. I shall move towards the second and more promising alternative by considering a major problem in the first.

I leave aside here the question of *who* might decide on the constituents of a framework, in order to concentrate on a question which must face any such decision-makers: on what grounds can the details of a framework be determined? If the proposing of a framework is *simply* the elevation into a privileged position of the pre-existing convictions of some particular persons or group, it can hardly fail to appear as an attempt to impose the favoured values of some on others. An alternative is to try to find some set of values which has an independent justification. By 'independent' I mean that the *grounds* on which the justification rests should not be simply the pre-existing convictions of some but not of all. (Notice that if there is an independent justification for some set of values, the fact that they are historically the values of one group becomes, if not irrelevant, at least less important.)

Now there is an area of activity which has been especially concerned with the justification of values — namely (parts of) moral and political philosophy. Can philosophy, then, show us what the values of the framework should be?

It is no surprise that the values to which the Committee refer are values of liberal democracy, since it is within the liberal tradition that the idea has developed of a society incorporating a diversity of values and goals within a common framework. I think it is still within that tradition that we are most likely to find guidance in determining a framework, not because I presuppose that liberalism has got it right, but just because the tradition has addressed itself directly to the relevant questions. There is, however, one aspect of much of the liberal tradition of political philosophy that could well be given up; I mean its abstract individualism.[9] Any theorizing applicable to a multicultural society must recognize the extent to which the identity of individuals is constituted by that which they inherit (including at least the initial basis of their values) from a cultural tradition or blend of traditions. Historically, the rootedness of persons in traditions has been more clearly recognized by critics of liberalism, on both the right and left.[10] But (simplifying drastically) it seems that conservative philosophies which have spoken to a condition in which a consensus within a tradition can be assumed, have said little on how a plurality of traditions can co-exist; while Marxian socialism, looking to a time when conflicts of interests will have been overcome, when perhaps 'a truly human morality'[11] will be possible, has not tried to articulate a framework of values for a condition in which conflicts of interests and values are still prevalent.

There is, then, some point in looking to liberal philosophy for the articulation of a framework, if we think of the persons to whom that framework applies not as free-floating individuals but as persons more or less firmly rooted in diverse practices and traditions. However, there is too great a diversity within liberal political philosophy for it to be possible to read off any single determinate framework.[12] Moreover, the normative recommendations made by particular philosophers depend heavily on the assumptions, including normative assumptions, that they put in. Nozick, for instance, in arguing for a minimal state framework, starts from a strong and undefended doctrine of individual rights; while Rawls, in his method of 'reflective equilibrium', deliberately selects assumptions which will tend to save in essentials what he takes to be the convictions of his readers. Since the values which are fed into liberal political philosophy will themselves be rooted in liberalism, an earlier problem re-emerges. Even if there is a determination within a society that a diversity of values — at a level not fundamental to the framework — should flourish, if the framework itself is constituted by and justified in terms of values which are part of a particular tradition — one especially prevalent historically in Britain and North America — we have not escaped the problem of imposition. We must still, then, pursue the question whether there can be an independent justification of some particular set and version of these values.

*   *   *

This brings us to ethical theory, the activity of articulating and attempting to justify some principle or set of principles which are taken to be morally fundamental, such that more specific moral positions can be justified in the light of them.[13] Within this area of theorizing there are particular ethical theories such as utilitarianism, or its most favoured contemporary rival, the view that individual rights are fundamental.[14] Moral philosophy seems as far as ever from consensus on any particular ethical theory. The lack of agreement, even if put down to the nature of academic philosophy, means that a particular theory cannot simply be read off for incorporation into a framework. There are, however, a few points that can usefully be made about tendencies in recent ethical theory.

First, the difficulties in the way of producing any independent justification of values have emerged clearly. Among other problems, the grounds of such a justification would have to be in some way genuinely universal. This cannot hold of many of the sorts of justification that have been proffered in the past. A theological grounding will not work when the relevant beliefs are not universally held; appeals to common moral consciousness, or to 'our' moral language, will not work for a similar reason. Even appeals to rationality or to human nature cannot simply assume that rationality or human nature are constants, independent of culture. Yet when appeal is made to something which does appear to be universal (as in Gewirth's attempt to ground a theory of rights in the fact of human action[15]) it is doubtful whether such a minimal basis can support anything sufficiently substantial.

Secondly, it is clear that there can be agreement on operative values at the level of a framework even where there is disagreement over the ultimate grounding of these values. Thus, theorists such as utilitarians who do not think that rights are *fundamental* in moral justification can agree with those who do, that at an *operative* level certain rights should be recognized.[16]

Thirdly, some ethical theorists have either argued that no independent justification can be had (so that, in Mackie's terms, morality can only be invented[17]), or have simply avoided raising the question of ultimate justification, in effect proposing a theory, not as being correct, but as being one that might reasonably be adopted.[18] Now it may appear that either of these last moves merely shifts the problem of justification; for it can now be asked, what reason do people have (particularly where their own values are rooted in a tradition other than that of the theory) for adopting one theory rather than another? But this is a very important shift. Perhaps it was a mistake to work with the idea of justification in the abstract, as if, whatever actual persons might think, there can be values which just *are justified*; the shift is to the idea of justification as a human activity, in which something has to be justified *to someone*. Our problem then shifts from looking for a set of values which has some independent justification, to looking for one that can be accepted as justified by all those to whom it is to be applied (whether or not they all have the same grounds for accepting it as justified).[19]

Something of this shift is embodied in contractualist ethical theories, such as those of Rawls and Scanlon.[20] Contractualism makes acceptability the criterion of justification, but in a hypothetical sense. The justification of principles is a function of whether they would be accepted —or, could not be rejected — by persons under certain conditions as a basis for co-existence; these conditions will minimally incorporate some notion of reasonableness, and may, as in Rawl's theory, be considerably stronger. This hypothetical aspect means that contractualism can be a rival to other ethical theories as a theory of what *is justified*, but also that, like others, it does not escape the question, what reason do persons have, given their own background of values, for accepting this theory? For it may be on a contractualist theory that certain principles are justified (because hypothetically acceptable) although many actual people reject them.[21] (And if certain persons object to being told that they ought to accept certain values because they have an independent philosophical justification, it will hardly help to be told that the justification consists in this, that they would accept these principles if they were being reasonable.)

*   *   *

This apparent impasse suggests that we should look, not at what would hypothetically be agreed, but at what can actually be agreed. We might speak of 'actual contractualism', but this will be a response to a practical problem rather than a rival ethical theory. The idea is that the nature of the framework should be a matter of negotiation between all those concerned. I have found in the philosophical literature little reference to actual negotiations rather than hypothetical agreement. An exception is J.L. Mackie. Agreeing with R.M. Hare that we need 'critical thinking' as a 'way of revising a community's working morality and of making adjustments when discrepant working moralities come into contact with one another'[22] he suggests that

> critical thinking might itself be a process of interaction, negotiation and debate between diverse groups with different starting points, different traditions of thought. Rather than proceeding *de haut en bas*, being pursued by one or more detached thinkers who try to stand above the whole conflict of interests and ideals, it would work up from below, from those conflicting views and claims themselves.
>
> In speaking of negotiation I mean real negotiation, conducted in the full light of day, while the parties retain their self-conscious individuality and divergent aims.[23]

Mackie, however, says nothing about the institutional setting in which such negotiation could take place. While I am far from being able to offer a blueprint, I shall try to inject some realism into Mackie's suggestion. I shall raise questions about the process of real negotiation under four headings:
1. What sorts of things can be negotiated?
2. What constraints, if any, should there be on the process?
3. In what institutional setting can real negotiation take place?
4. How can negotiation of values be effective in relation to the actual political workings of our society?

*   *   *

1. If the idea of negotiating values seems puzzling in itself, this may be because of the difficulty of getting away from an implicitly objectivist, or realist, idea of moral values. Roughly, in so far as we hold our values as true, we will not think that they can be opened up to negotiation, any more than the truth about the motions of the planets could be settled by negotiation (though some theses of epistemological relativism might give us pause even on this). Will there not be some moral convictions on which I, or you, or anyone will not be prepared to negotiate? How, then, should we assess the suggestion which Marcus Singer has drawn from William James,

> that what is morally right or wrong — the rights and duties of the various parties to an actual controversy or conflict — can be determined, and morally ought to be determined, by a process of negotiation, bargaining, or compromise[24]..?

In approaching this suggestion, Singer has usefully distinguished 'moral problems', 'moral issues' and 'social problems'.[25] There is no suggestion that all the moral problems faced by individuals must be opened up to society-wide negotiation. But from time to time it comes to public attention that there exist in society strong differences of opinion about the morality of some sort of action. Then there is a moral *issue*; and further 'for every issue on which opinion is inflamed, in which the controversy gets worse and degenerates into conflict ... the *society* has a problem, the problem of how best to resolve the issue'[26] — which is itself a moral problem on a different level. While a pluralist society by definition can live with some moral issues, it has to be able to resolve or at least to contain those which become social problems — and to do this is part of the role of a framework of values.

In an actual dispute, then, the parties come with their pre-existing beliefs and commitments, otherwise there would be no dispute. Of course one cannot expect that these will simply be suspended. There are, however, at least two things which can still take place in a process of negotiation: (a) the parties may come to understand and see the force in each other's positions, and with this understanding they may shift towards each other in their *moral* positions, so that they end up, if not agreeing, at any rate less diametrically opposed; (b) even if they do not shift in their fundamental moral positions, they may be able to reach a compromise on working principles to govern what is actually to be done — something which, for each party, will be worse than its own ideal but better than the other party's ideal.

If such a compromise can be reached, it is plausible to say that, in the existing circumstances, the outcome of the compromise *is* what ought to be done; and in this sense we can accept Singer's suggestion.

Now if such a process of negotiation makes sense over particular moral issues, it makes sense also over the constituents of a framework; indeed many of the disagreements over the constituents of our existing approximation to a framework *are* moral issues.[27] A framework, then, cannot be above negotiation. Moreover, it is important that the framework should not be treated as above negotiation; for if it were, in Britain at present this would amount to the majority group taking an assimilationist attitude regarding the framework, expecting others to adopt it though they have had no say in its formulation.

*   *   *

2. It may be thought that even if the framework is negotiable, there must be some ground rules for any actual process of negotiation. This can be accepted, though even such ground rules will be subject to alteration, through negotiation again, from one time and context to another. The existing traditions in this society are not lacking in resources from which provisional ground rules for negotiation can be drawn. Suggestions can also be drawn from philosophical writings which may be applicable for this purpose. Mackie suggests as a ground rule 'equality of sacrifices in compromises between our Lockean rights'.[28] This is possibly taken from Ackerman, who proposes a set of principles centring on the notion of neutrality between conceptions of the good.[29] Also relevant is Habermas's postulation of an ideal speech situation, the features of which must be anticipated in actual situations.[30]

Probably more important than any particular ground rules are some general conditions brought out by Bernard Williams:[31] in particular, that the parties are resolved to reach an agreement. Where divisions within a society are very great, there is least likely to be this resolve; but where they are not *too* great, education may be able to do something to promote the willingness and preparedness to negotiate.

Another important point which I cannot deal with here, is that in any actual negotiation the parties will be unequal in power (in part because the prevailing ideology will be supportive of some rather than others). So far as possible the ground rules, and the institutional channels, must be designed so as to minimize the effects of such inequalities.

*   *   *

3. In what forum can effective negotiation take place, when the issue is the framework of values for a whole society? The current political system, working through the party system and majority voting, for the most part does not function in this way, and in any case is far from representative of the cultural traditions which should be involved in the negotiation. Further, to think of representation at all overlooks a vital part of the case for 'actual contractualism': the attempt to arrive at values which can be accepted *by everyone*.

There is no reason in principle why new fora should not be devised which would involve far more of the population. The possibilities and drawbacks here would largely parallel those discussed under the heading of participatory democracy. However, I want to propose that *schools* should not merely equip young people to participate, at some later date, in negotiation of values, but should themselves be a locus of this negotiation. Before considering likely objections to this idea, I shall mention two points in its favour.

First, schools are the only institution in our society which virtually everyone goes through, coming into contact in the process with at least some diversity of others. Further, the fact that in different schools there are different mixes of elements of the population may go some slight way to counteract imbalances in the population as a whole, by ensuring that minority groups will have a preponderance of numbers in some particular negotiating contexts.[32]

Secondly, actual negotiation in schools could give a firmer grounding to the general (but, as pointed out above, not universal) assumption that individuals in a democracy are morally obliged to obey the law, and perhaps also in less tangible ways to go along with the system. This obligation is usually assumed to apply, perhaps from early adolescence, and certainly from the time of legal adulthood, so that (despite the rhetoric of consent) people are being expected to abide by that in which they have not yet had any say at all.[33] It seems appropriate that persons should have a part in negotiating the framework of their rights and duties within the few years preceding their legal adulthood.

The major objection to this proposal is likely to be that persons in the

latter years of compulsory schooling are too immature and inexperienced to negotiate the framework of their society. A full answer to this
would require the development of many points which I can only mention here:

(a) It could not in fact be the case that the whole framework of society was
remade with each year group passing through the schools; the power of
negotiation is limited. I consider below how it can nevertheless have
some effect.

(b) If the objection is that sixteen-year-olds are not rational autonomous
persons, but will simply bring into negotiation the prejudices of their
parents or peer group, this misses the point. Negotiation does not require
that the negotiators be autonomous individuals, if that means persons
somehow detached from any tradition. On the contrary, it presupposes
that people bring their prejudices into the negotiation.[34]

(c) As for young people being inexperienced in the ways of the world, the
force of this point is ambivalent. Experience can lead people to revise
their values, but it can also make prejudices more entrenched; and very
frequently people give up on early ideals. A stage at which people are
aware of the problems they imminently face without yet being too directly oppressed by them may be no bad time for negotiation on
fundamentals.[35]

(d) I have not suggested that schools should be the only forum for
negotiation, nor that adults should not also be involved in negotiation in
schools; community schools could make this possible.

(e) The earlier years of education could prepare people for their role as
negotiators in the last year or so of compulsory schooling. This would
become an important aspect of moral and political education and would
have spin-off benefits beyond the actual process of negotiation.

(f) A suggestion of this nature can only be adequately assessed through
fuller specification of the proposal, discussion in the light of experience,
and attempts at implementation, which initially could be piecemeal.

*   *   *

4. In terms of the reasons for proposing negotiation over values, the
danger is that such a process might be seen as having *only* educational
value, considerable though that might be. The question remains: can
negotiation have an actual effect on the framework of a society?

The full framework is to be of values, practices and procedures: thus it will include both laws and deliberately created institutions, as well as less tangible attitudes of individuals. The latter may in fact be directly affected through negotiation. As regards the former, a framework cannot be created from scratch even once, let alone repeatedly. This is not simply a matter of realism about the possibility of change; a set of values, practices and procedures cannot constitute a framework without a degree of stability over time. Both in practice and in principle, then, the approximation to a framework that we have has to be the starting point, but it is to be seen as open to modification, with the possibility through its progressive modification of a wider consensus than currently exists.

The proposal is not, then, that the many separate negotiations going on in different schools must somehow be co-ordinated into a blueprint. Rather, negotiation in schools will be a critical forum. In some cases, no doubt, it will effect no change, not because everyone is satisfied, but because no agreement is reached. In others, it may result in a more free and informed consent to, and consensus on, elements of existing practice and values. But it may also result in an agreed and expressed dissatisfaction with elements of current practice and values. If it turns out that the outcomes of many separate negotiations point together towards certain revisions in the framework, it should not be impossible for this result to have influence through more conventional political channels (which will themselves be open to change and extension).

*   *   *

Three points in conclusion.

First, the arguments and ideas in this paper are only a sketch, leaving many unanswered questions which I hope that I and others can contribute to answering.

Secondly, there are those to whom my suggestion will seem to involve the use of schools for something quite other than their proper purpose. But if that purpose is education, what can be more educational than the learning and mutual understanding that must be involved in a process of negotiation rather than confrontation or subordination? If the objection is that my suggestion is too close to that political education which critics have accused of being indoctrinatory,[36] I would reply that the attempt to get people, of whatever ethnic and cultural background, to fit into some given framework of values, comes far closer to indoctrination.

Lastly, I am aware that my proposal might seem to add yet another burden to hard-pressed teachers. In fact, on two conditions, I think it offers an opportunity to be welcomed by teachers as professional educators. The conditions are that teachers be properly prepared for the role of facilitators of negotiation over values, and that their contribution in this way, and in others, to the well-being of a pluralist society be properly recognised by the rest of that society.

Notes

1. Swann Report, 1985, ch.1, para.1.
2. Ibid., ch.1, para.4.
3. For the most part I shall speak of 'values' rather than 'values, practices and procedures', partly as shorthand, partly because it is the value component of a framework with which I am most concerned in this chapter. Values do not, of course, exist in the abstract, but are both embodied within, and may be better or worse realized by, different practices and procedures; but I cannot go into the interconnections here.
4. Ibid., ch.1, para.2.
5. Ibid., ch.1, para.4.
6. Ibid.
7. For examples of philosophical arguments which allow that disobedience can be democratic, cf. Singer, P. (1973); Rawls (1972), ch.6; Dworkin (1977), ch.8.
8. Cf. MacIntyre (1981), ch.17.
9. Cf. Lukes (1973), ch.9.
10. For recent examples of such criticism cf. MacIntyre (1981), Sandel (1982).
11. The phrase is that of Engels. Cf. Tucker (1972) pp.667-8 (from *Anti-Dühring*)
12. I have in mind the differences between, say, Rawls (1972), Dworkin (1977), and Nozick (1974); the last-named is hardly liberal, but certainly individualist.
13. For a fuller definition, of *an* ethical theory, cf. Williams (1985), p.72. I have discussed more fully the possible role of ethical theory in forming the framework of a pluralist society in Haydon (1986).
14. For the debate between utilitarianism and rights-based theory, cf. many of the articles in Frey (1985), Paul et al. (1984), Waldron (1984).
15. Gewirth (1977, 1984).
16. Cf. Gray (1984); and the debate between Mackie and Hare in Frey (1985).
17. Mackie (1977).

18. A good example is Scheffler (1982).
19. For a related line of thought cf. Waldron (1984), pp.19-20.
20. Rawls (1972); Scanlon (1982).
21. Cf. Scanlon (1982), p.116.
22. Mackie in Frey (1985), p.97.
23. Ibid. (1985), p.100.. Cf. Mackie (1977), pp.93, 235-9.
24. Singer, M. (1985), p.21.
25. Ibid., pp.12-13.
26. Ibid., p.13.
27. See above, p.26.
28. Mackie in frey (1985), p.100.
29. Ackerman (1980).
30. Habermas (1976). Cf. the articles by Thompson and by Lukes in Thompson and Held (1982).
31. Williams (1985), p.99.
32. The possibility that schools offer of negotiation involving — over time — the whole population seems to be an argument in favour of compulsory schooling. For the difficulty in justifying this in individualistic terms cf. Haydon (1977).
33. I have explored this problem in Haydon (1979). Cf. Pateman (1979).
34. The recognition of the universality of prejudices, or prejudgements, owed in part to Gadamer, is vital here. Cf. the chapter by Malcolm Jones in this volume.
35. In being able to make only limited and uncertain assumptions about their future life prospects, young people are to a degree behind a 'veil of ignorance' — though not nearly as thick a veil as that described by Rawls (1972).
36. Cf. Scruton et al. (1985).

Prejudice

Malcolm Jones

I shall contend here that the account of the concept of prejudice given in the Swann Report (1985) is inadequate and that as a consequence the possibility of a genuinely educational approach to the problems which prejudice raises for life in a pluralist society is overlooked. Through discussion of the report's analysis I shall argue for an account of prejudice that indicates the appropriateness of the educational approach I have in mind.[1]

The report characterizes prejudice as 'a preconceived opinion or bias for or against someone or something' (ch.2, para.2.1). Prejudices are seen as tending to be 'rigid, immutable and irreversible' (ibid.), and are contrasted with preferences which are said to be 'generally open to reason and thus to change' (ibid.).

At this point some confusion appears. In the main text of the report the asserted rigidity of prejudice is explained by reference to prejudgements. Something is said to have been prejudged if it has been 'evaluated on the basis of assumed characteristics in advance and, by implication, without adequate information on which to base a rational judgement' (ibid.).

Prejudgement is represented as approaching the world with a rigidly pre-set way of looking which remains unmodified and unmodifiable in the light of experience and hence appears to be irrational. But a footnote (p.13) quotes Banton who distinguishes between prejudgement and prejudice by saying: 'Prejudgements becomes prejudices only if they are not subject to modification in the light of experience.'

This is more subtle than the main text; now prejudgement is not seen as unavoidably rigid. Banton suggests that holding prejudgements is not necessarily exceptional so long as we are conscious of their nature and are willing to change them in the light of experience. Prejudgements become prejudices only when they are held rigidly and the possibility of modification in the light of experience is lost. Thus Banton allows what the main text seems to discount: the possibility that one might rationally hold prejudgements.

*   *   *

The notion of *prejudgement* needs explication.[1] This will require us to look at the foundations of the public conceptions by which we make sense of the world. The customary practices and modes of judgement of every human form of life tacitly presuppose certain 'facts' to which members of a form of life come tacitly to acquiesce in the course of their early socialization. These are the culturally-vouched-for prejudgements in terms of which members of any particular culture or subculture make sense of their experience, the foundations of their culture's world view. Some of these prejudgements (e.g. the assumption of the genetic 'superiority' of white over black 'races') may be open to criticism in terms of truth and logical coherence. But other more foundational prejudgements, I shall argue, have their origins in traditional cosmologies, traditional views of the cosmos and humanity's place in it, which are not easily assessed in such terms. In a culturally pluralist society we must expect cross-cultural disagreement to occur which is the result of mismatch at the level of foundational prejudgement and a rational approach to the resolution of this sort of culture-clash must involve principles beyond those of truth and logic.

I shall say more about these wider principles later. My first tasks must be to elucidate the meaning of 'foundational prejudgement', to show that different cultural traditions *do* presuppose different foundational prejudgements and to justify my assertion that debate on the truth of such prejudgements is unlikely to be of use in resolving cross-cultural disagreement.

Strawson, in the introduction to his book *Individuals*, distinguishes two strands in metaphysics:

> Descriptive metaphysics is content to describe the actual structure of our thought about the world, revisionary metaphysics is concerned to produce a better structure.[2]

The aim of descriptive metaphysics is to dig beneath the surface of our language use to discover the concepts and categories which are the foundations of our everyday modes of judgement. Revisionist metaphysics is concerned with critical reflection on those foundations and with '. . . furthering or registering new directions or styles of thought'. But, as Strawson goes on to say,

> . . . it would be a great blunder to think of metaphysics only in this historical style. For there is a massive central core of human thinking which has no history- or none recorded in the history of thought; there are categories and concepts which, in their most fundamental character, change not at all. Obviously, these are not the specialities of the most refined thinking. They are the commonplaces of the least refined thinking; and are yet the indispensable core of the conceptual equipment of the most sophisticated human beings. It is with these, their interconnexions, and the structure they form, that a descriptive metaphysics will be primarily concerned.[3]

For Strawson, descriptive metaphysics is concerned with isolating fundamental categories of human thought, notions like time, space, object, person. For my purposes here I wish to suggest that although the basic categories of human thought may correspond (or show a close family resemblance) across cultures, nevertheless the actual concepts in use in different cultures will exhibit important differences.

What I am suggesting does not amount to out-and-out cultural relativism. If we take certain important human concepts, for instance the concept of a person, we shall find a 'core conception' common to all cultures, but that the concept in actual use in any culture will be considerably richer than this common core.

Strawson's conception of a person as an embodied subject of experience is one which, I believe, captures a part of every human culture's conception. But any particular culture's conception of a person is wider than this, is enriched by other notions which have their origins in that culture's traditional cosmology, its traditional account of the cosmos and our place in it.

The concept of a person in Hindu culture reflects the Vedantic cosmology. Within this tradition the individual self (or ego) is seen as an illusion caused by desire. By proper discipline we can dispel this illusion and become aware of our innermost Self which is Atman, the immanent aspect of God. Thus, through loss of the ego, we can come joyfully to experience the essential unity of all things and our oneness with God.[4] Such a conception has implications for the notion of personal development and indicates the appropriateness of spending a part of one's life in asceticism and meditation. It is not unusual for successful Hindu men of the world to do just this in their later years.

The Islamic conception of a person reflects the cosmology of the Qur'an. Each of us is seen as a now-embodied soul possessing, by God's grace, both free will and almost limitless potentialities. God also gives us guidance, through the revelation of the Qur'an, for our self-development. Since we have free will our self-development involves us in disciplining ourselves so as to follow God's guidance. Islam emphasizes that self-development occurs in the world and in society and therefore the task of the Islamic community is to create a social order in which each individual's opportunities for self-development are optimally facilitated.[5] This is why Qur'anic interpretation is fundamental to both the political and legal process in Islamic societies. It is also the reason why, for Islam, the idea of keeping religion out of politics is simply absurd.

In the secular West we are strongly influenced by the cosmology which underpins physics, in which God has become irrelevant and the universe is seen as a physical system governed by principles which the enquiring mind can come to understand. By using this understanding we can act to achieve our desired ends. Thus our everyday conception of a person is of an entity which desires certain ends, calculates efficient means, and acts in order to achieve the desired ends. The notion of self-development which goes with this conception is essentially one of gain: gain in knowledge related to technical mastery over the world (both physical and social), gain in wealth and status, and gain in material possessions. The thinness of this conception is apparent to many of us and is evinced by the difficulty we have in establishing any substantive moral philosophy in our secular lives.

All these examples are drastically over simplified and do not reflect the diversity within or the relations between the traditions sketched. But as illustrations they are adequate for the purpose of indicating that the actual concepts of a person which dominate the public life of different cultures, are, in fact, different (although, as I have said, not unrelated). They show that different conceptions drawn from different cosmologies dominate different cultures, in the sense that they underpin the modes of reasoning which dominate the relevant cultures, into which members are initiated during early socialization. In this way the relevant conceptions dominate the public life of any culture simply by underpinning the modes of reasoning which carry weight (i.e. are found persuasive by) the majority of that culture's members.

Thus, traditional cosmologies influence the everyday lives of people in different cultures, even if those people know little or nothing about them. They do this by providing the foundational prejudgements of influential modes of reasoning. This is why Qur'anic interpretation remains a potent force in political debate in Islamic societies, whereas in the materialistic West economic arguments tend to carry the day.[6]

Influential cosmologies provide basic categories and concepts of thought combined to form sets of metaphysical and ontological prejudgements, the pre-understandings which are further interpreted and elaborated as we seek to extend our understanding. These are the foundational prejudgements of various cultures, ways of looking at, and ways of making sense of, the world.

Such foundational prejudgements are the bed-rock of our various culturally-vouched-for ways of understanding our experience. They are not totally inaccessible to revision, indeed history shows us that many of them have been revised. But such revision can only take place against a background of foundational prejudgements which are not found problematic, which provide the 'safe ground' of agreement from which disagreement can be resolved.

This possibility of piecemeal reform makes it logically possible that revisionary metaphysics might one day revise the diversity of foundational prejudgements found in our diverse cultures so as to provide a unified set of foundational prejudgements which would underpin a truly universal human culture. But this would be a long-term project and the long history of revisionary metaphysics indicates that such a project would be unlikely to come to fruition soon enough to allow us to use its findings to resolve the problems of cultural diversity in a pluralistic context here and now. So revisionary metaphysics is unlikely to help with the problems of cultural pluralism. We have to try to deal with the problems of cultural mismatch at the level of foundational prejudgements in a different way.

*   *   *

The basic problem of culturally pluralist societies is that citizens from different cultural backgrounds tend to enter public debate with reasoned arguments constructed in different culturally-vouched-for styles and based on different foundational prejudgements. The result is the occurrence of cross-cultural debates in which culturally-different participants will fail to be persuaded by arguments which, in their cultures of origin, would be found persuasive.

In the United Kingdom context this could be very dangerous indeed. If the majority culture simply continues to make public policy decisions on the basis of its established modes of reasoning, members of minority cultures are likely to find themselves disenfranchised, their culturally-conditioned interests and concerns being simply ignored. It is the basis for institutional racism which, intentional or not, has already led to feelings of resentment and alienation amongst members of minority cultural groups.

Part of the solution to this problem must be, as the Swann Report makes clear (ch.6), to widen the curricula of our schools so as to give all pupils a better understanding of the prejudgemental foundations of all the cultures which make up our society. This follows from the unreflective and habitual nature of much human life and the problems which occur when culturally different groups, unreflectively following their habitual patterns of judgement and practice, simply collide. This needs a little explanation.

In the process of being socialized into our home forms of life we all acquire habits of judgement and response which range from our grasp of our native language to our capacity to accord with established norms of interpersonal etiquette.[8] We acquire much of our understanding of our home form of life and our place in it in the process of acquiring habitual strategies which facilitate the achievement of our desired ends in that context.

In most everyday contexts, the strategies by which we achieve our ends most surely are those which do not fly in the face of the established traditions of judgement and practice which are the norms against which others judge our activities to be acceptable or not. Thus, in finding our way by trial and error in our home cultures, we acquire a tacit (i.e. not easily accessible to conscious reflection) grasp of its traditions and the foundational prejudgements which underpin them.

In a pluralist society the tacit nature of most people's grasp of their 'cultural roots' is a dangerous source of cross-cultural misunderstanding. Mistakes arise as people of one culture interpret the actions of people of a different culture by looking at them in inappropriate ways.

Knowledge of our own and others' foundational prejudgements and their implications for everyday practice and judgement would at least enable us to understand the source of many cross-cultural disagreements and to avoid dangerous and unnecessary misunderstandings. So, bringing our own and others' tacit prejudgements to conscious awareness does seem to be an important element in any education designed to equip citizens of diverse cultural backgrounds to live and work together in some sort of functioning harmony.

But the problem of agreeing on important (to all citizens) matters of public policy remains. Understanding does not imply agreement. Although some differences in culturally-vouched-for prejudgements might be resolved by argument based on principles of truth and logic, not all differences in prejudgements are likely to be resolved in this way. To expect considerations of truth and logic to resolve all conflicts between foundational prejudgements would be to expect revisionary metaphysics suddenly to achieve a greater success than it has over several thousand years. This is not, as I said earlier, logically impossible, but it is a monumental practical improbability.

We must, then, expect culture clash to occur at the level of what might be called foundational cosmological prejudgements, our diverse beliefs about the nature of the self, the existence, or not, of God (and in the former case, His nature). And such beliefs are notoriously intractable to demonstrations of truth and falsity. Since argument about the truth and coherence of prejudgements at this foundational level is likely to prove fruitless, I suggest that the rational course would be formally to identify them as rationally tenable but contingently undecidable foundational prejudgements.

To do this would be to accept that it can be rational to hold prejudements which cannot be shown to be true. This is not problematic because the sort of prejudgements under discussion are the very foundations of our capacity to understand anything at all. It could hardly be rational to abandon our capacity to understand.

But it would seem just as irrational to cling to such prejudgements, refusing to consider modifying or reinterpreting them at all (which is possible so long as it is done piecemeal fashion). As any society changes through time, the implications which traditional prejudgements have for the nature of the good life might cease to facilitate congenial (to the populace) social living and themselves become bones of contention. Since we cannot 'opt out' of history, it can hardly be rational to hold any particular prejudgement so rigidly that we refuse to allow that what was once rationally tenable has been rendered untenable by historical change.

Such problems surely have to be faced up to by any rational person. They are potentially destructive of community and are unavoidable in any society undergoing a change from a more homogeneous to a more heterogeneous (i.e. pluralist) cultural composition. All cultures change through time, even those based on prejudgements believed to be divine revelation — scriptures can be, and often are, reinterpreted.

So now it might seem irrational either to abandon wholesale or to cling rigidly to the foundational prejudgements of any cultural tradition. But we can escape this apparent dilemma by changing our attitude to our cultures' traditions, by adopting a stance of 'why not?' to them. We should formally confer the status of 'true' on (contingently) undecidable foundational prejudgements for so long as the traditions which presuppose them facilitate congenial living.

Only if, in the light of experience, we find the dictates of tradition directing us where we deem it inadvisable to go should we remove the procedural immunity from critique granted to them and turn to reflection on how to replace or modifiy or reinterpret them. This, I suggest, is the sense in which it is rational to operate in everyday life on the basis of (contingently) undecidable prejudgements.

Where experience throws our foundational prejudgements into question we must reflect. But, as I have argued, we must be careful about making our objective one of establishing incontrovertible and universal prejudgemental foundations — this would be to expect too much of revisionary metaphysics. In many cases we must be satisfied with aiming to achieve agreed prejudgements of a sort adequate for the establishment of particular public policies which will command the willing and unresentful assent of a large majority of citizens from all cultural backgrounds.

The establishment of such a consensus is likely to require compromise, but it is essential if a society is to be capable of communal action on problems which affect all citizens and if it is to function as home for all its members. There is a presupposition here, which I believe to be unproblematic, that feeling at home in the society in which one lives is a basic human good. Feeling at home where one lives seems a very basic biological need in social animals like ourselves. Empirical evidence that this is so can be found in many great works of literature and in the massive literature on alienation across several disciplines.

* * *

Prejudgement is a basic feature of human understanding. Particular prejudgements are beliefs which are held despite the lack of any demonstration of their truth. Without some prejudgements it seems impossible that we could make very much sense at all of our experience.

From the perspective of formal logic, particular *prejudices* also appear as undischarged assumptions and can be seen to have a similar epistemological role to prejudgements. But 'prejudice' carries with it more than the epistemological significance of 'prejudgement'. As we have seen, nothing in the notion of prejudgement implies unalterability in the light of experience. 'Prejudice', however, carries such connotations. Thus 'prejudice' must be read not as a term of epistemology, but rather as a psychological term.

When we identify an individual's prejudgements as prejudices we are not making an epistemological point about the status of beliefs. Rather, we are making a psychological point about a person: that for some reason 'this' person believes *in* the truth of 'these' prejudgements in a way that makes it especially difficult for him or her to question their tenability in the light of experience. This amounts to saying that, relative to relevant prejudgements, the person is resistant to requests to reflect critically on their tenability.

This amounts to identifying prejudice as a psychological phenomenon characterized by unquestioning belief *in* relevant prejudgements. To understand more about prejudice we must now ask what, in practice, might militate against the adoption of what I have argued to be the rational attitude to the prejudgements of our cultural traditions.

One possibility is that the tacit prejudgements (both foundational and other) of tradition, once made explicit, might be blankly asserted to be true, with the consequence that any different set of prejudgements (e.g. those of any other culture) would be asserted to be false in so far as they are inconsistent with the preferred prejudgemental basis. This usually amounts to an unjustifiable attempt at cultural imperialism since the preferred prejudgements will be derived from a particular culture and their assertion as true will amount to the assertion (in some unspecifiable sense) of the superiority of that culture over all others. This would involve making claims about the truth of foundational cosmological prejudgements which, as I argued in the previous section, are unlikely to be supportable by any adequate argument. Thus, to assert the prejudgements of 'this' or 'that' culture's traditions to be unquestionably (by all virtuous and right-minded people) true, is to retreat from reason into a rigid mentality which transforms living and 'evolving' traditions into static and stagnant ideologies: systems of belief unjustifiably asserted to be true which serve to license the perpetuation of customary but otherwise unjustifiable traditions of judgement and practice.[9]

This pushes us to the question of why anyone should prefer an ideology which perpetuates problems to rational compromise designed to eliminate them. The answer to this question is: prejudice. But, I suggest, the central problem is not prejudice against others. The problem arises from the positive prejudice in favour of the traditions of our home culture which many of us have, a prejudice which is at once both valuable and potentially dangerous.

Unreflective living is very attractive to many human beings (of *all* cultures). Fromm, in his *Fear of Freedom*,[10] reported forty years ago that many people react to an increased scope for autonomous choice with increased fear, anxiety and insecurity. Such people are happiest when they can 'switch on the autopilot of habit' and function smoothly without encountering any circumstances which require them to reflect on their own prejudgements. When faced with the potential misunderstandings which are always present in communication with others who do not share one's own prejudgements, such people tend to respond with incomprehension, fear and dislike. Thus one aspect of prejudice is fear of what is culturally and prejudgementally other.

But prejudice has a less fearful aspect. The comfort and pleasure which we can derive from indulgence in what is familiar is not in itself exceptionable. For me, raised as a Nonconformist Christian, the sound of the hymn 'Jerusalem' conjures images of Miss Nettleton's room in my primary school and of St. John's church where I sang (and chewed gum and played 'noughts and crosses') in the choir. Rodrigo's guitar concerto 'd'Aranjuez' brings other memories, of a bed-sit in Islington and a good and loving companion. Handel's *Messiah* evokes still fonder memories.

This is to say that the juxtaposition (in my experience) of these 'artefacts' of my home culture with personally significant events in my life has led to the forging of strong sentimental ties with certain features of my home culture. The point of these reminiscences is to show that I am, in an important sense, prejudiced in favour of a great many features of my home form of life. I know that there is great cultural variation in the use of 'please' and 'thank you' and that people of both Asian and West Indian origin don't use these words in the same way as the indigenous English do.[11] But I still feel more at home when 'pleased' and 'thank-youed' in the manner to which my rearing accustomed me.

This prejudice is my sentimental attachment to home. It is such shared sentimental attachment that constitutes the community of sentiment which is an essential element in the fabric of any genuine community. A West Indian Baptist might have similar prejudices in favour of a certain style of religious service, feeling the services of English Baptists to be rather cold-blooded and spiritless affairs.

Most of us are to some extent prejudiced in favour of home in a way which is natural, socially valuable, and a source of great comfort. I could follow the Swann report and call what I am talking of here preference rather than prejudice. But this is too nice a distinction and risks obscuring the crucial point. Most of us are most comfortable with the pre-judgements of home; despite all disagreements, home is where the heart is. Being at home elicits feelings of belonging and security which are very important to us, feelings which make it difficult to question the pre-judgements of the traditions of our home form of life.

To abandon those prejudgements is to render ourselves incapable of truly going home to the feelings home elicits for so long as we adhere to its traditions. When we dissent from the traditional modes of judgement and practice of our home communities we find ourselves unavoidably in conflict with our own habits: those ingrained habits of feeling and response acquired during early socialization. This means we are likely to find our conscious decisions at odds with our deepest tacit beliefs and emotional responses. The result will be confusion, loss of assuredness and often self-doubt (the authority of health education textbooks often pales when set against the authority of priests on such issues as masturbation, sex before marriage, etc.).

The difficulty of coping with these feelings of confusion is well known. It was awareness of this difficulty that made the Jesuits confident that if a child is given into their care for the first seven years of life (s)he is likely to remain safely within the fold thereafter. Psychotherapists know that an important aspect of their work is to help people overcome such emotional barriers and bring the tacit understandings 'programmed-in' during socialization to focal awareness in readiness to assess and, where necessary, modify them.

Such phenomena are familiar from everyday life, not merely from its psychopathology. They are manifestations of our sentimental attachment to home, our prejudice in favour of the traditions of home. My contention is that we must acknowledge such prejudice as a central aspect of human Being. We cannot abandon such prejudices without making very painful and disquieting changes within ourselves.

This transforms the notion of prejudice. It grants that it is rational for us, being the sort of animal we are, to allow ourselves prejudices. In particular it is rational for us to remain prejudiced in favour of the traditions of our home form of life for so long as we acknowledge those prejudices to be no more (*and* no less) than historically explicable features of our emotional lives. What is not rational is the 'forgetfulness of Being' which leads us to assert our prejudices to be unquestionably true and hence leads to ideological conflict. Which is to say that with prejudices, as with prejudgements, the rational attitude is one of, 'why not?'

We can only resist the drift towards ideological conflict and its 'resolution' by imposition of the views of the powerful upon the relatively powerless by acknowledging the universality of prejudice, the fact that human beings tend to forge sentimental links with the prejudgements of home which can make it difficult for us (for reasons of our emotional responses) genuinely to reflect on their justifiability. This acknowledgement of the universality of prejudice is a necessary step towards being able to *manage* prejudice and to eliminate socially unacceptable (because they are destructive of the possibility of a genuinely pluralist *community*) prejudices, for instance the prejudice against members of other forms of life which results from the fearful rejection (usually involving their characterization as stupid or wicked) of people whose prejudgements and prejudices are different from our own.

*   *   *

Once the universality of prejudice is accepted we can *hold a conversation* between members of different cultures based on the idea that we are all emotionally tied to culturally-vouched-for prejudgements some of the most crucial (to our world views) of which we cannot (as a matter of contingent fact) show to be true. The aim of such a conversation would be that the participants should work towards understanding one another as emotionally committed members of various forms of life, together with some understanding of what it is that each is committed to, what each sees as important social issues, how crucial that importance is and why.[12]

Beyond this the conversation would be aimed at encouraging people to work towards compromise in the light not only of what they know of other cultures' practices, but also of what they know of how members of those cultures feel about those practices. Working towards agreed prejudgements which everybody would feel able to adopt in the interests of social stability would be seen as a process of willing compromise necessary for the creation and maintenance of a pluralist community in which everyone could feel at home, agree on important communal problems and work in a unified, co-operative manner to resolve them.

By 'adopt' here I do not mean 'come to believe in'. Rather that people should agree to operate on the basis of such a compromise in the interests of social stability. Initially this would be difficult because it would involve our acting against our inclinations, feelings and beliefs in some circumstances. It seems to me, however, that if we could make such compromise work, it is likely that people would get used to particular compromises and move towards adopting the agreed principles at the deeper level of belief (on the perfectly rational principle that the proof of the pudding is in the eating). And, of course, later generations, raised in a society functioning smoothly on the basis of cross-cultural compromise, would be likely to come to see compromise in the interests of social stability as entirely 'natural'.

The establishment of an on-going conversation between cultures is the only way for a pluralistic society to avoid degeneration into warring factions. Apartheid, leaving aside its moral abhorrence, is evidently unstable. Repatriation is not workable (where does one send a black Londoner 'back' to?) and the pretence that it might be, besides being mendacious, distracts from the necessity of getting on with coping with the de facto pluralism in which we live (I'm thinking here primarily of the context of the United Kingdom). It seems to me that school is the place where people should be given the understanding and the personal and social skills necessary for participation in such conversation. The existence of the problem suggests that such understanding is not typically transmitted in the informal education we all receive at home. In what follows I shall expand on this notion of *education for conversation*.

*   *   *

The sort of discussion required is not designed to get at any truths except about the participants: their opinions, what really matters to them, where they 'come from' culturally speaking. Of course any truths agreed by all parties would be treated as such, but what those truths are is to be discovered in the process of conversation, not brought to it as unacknowledged prejudgement or prejudice.

In the school context a wide range of topics already covered (often using discussion approaches) would provide suitable objects for discussion: sex, marriage, the family, the rights and duties of children and parents, crime and punishment... The discussion would go beyond the discovery of facts about different cultures and how they differ (the multicultural education approach). The central aim would be to arrive at information on cultural difference in prejudgement by way of addressing the prejudices of the participants.

A more multicultural mainstream curriculum in which students were made more aware of the foundational prejudgements and the underlying cosmologies of different cultural traditions would, of course, facilitate this conversational approach. And the conversational approach would enhance the teaching about different traditions simply by transforming what might otherwise be perceived (by students) as inert information into information about how real people, living real lives, actually perceive themselves and the world. It would engage students' attention and make the information more relevant to them.

In this new sort of discussion any clash of opinion is not merely something to be smoothed over, it is something to be looked at so as to bring out the underlying disagreement in prejudgement and to relate that disagreement back to the various traditions which have authority for the different participants. Each participant, in expressing his/her views on relevant issues, would also encounter the more familiar problems of maintaining internal coherence and of facing up to questions about whether (s)he really does want to assert explicitly 'this' or 'that' hitherto hidden assumption (including those which are racist or potentially so). By careful question and answer and by restating a respondent's replies to her or his satisfaction, the participants will acquire a deeper understanding of one another as emotionally committed members of different forms of life. They will also become sensitized to the problems inherent in cross-cultural discussion and acquire some skill in its practice.

In the clashes of opinion which must occur in such discussion we find the opportunity to bring the tacit prejudgements we carry with us from home (often as prejudices) to focal awareness and hence make them accessible to critical reflection in the light of experience. Thus each participant will gain important self knowledge. Further, an understanding of people from other cultural backgrounds will be acquired which will undermine the 'otherness' of other cultures. In slowly grasping the significance of the universality of prejudice as indicating something universal about human beings *qua* human beings, participants will increasingly begin to 'see through' the surface variety to the humanity underneath (those elements in human life which become more the same the more they change). Likings for two foods will be seen as essentially the same thing when both dishes are grasped as 'treats for special occasions' — often religious festivals. It will emerge that everybody agrees that things like politeness and treating people with proper respect are important, but that different cultures disagree on the actual form of proper politeness-rituals and on exactly who commands respect and why.

But it remains central to my proposal here that the process by which such information is acquired is just as important as the information itself. The process involved is one of controlled and therefore fruitful inter-cultural conflict in which disagreements are valuable occasions upon which important understandings can be achieved and dangerous (because we would rather avoid the consequences) misunderstandings avoided. Taking part in the process will teach the practical skills needed for it and (if I am correct) the value of being careful in initial dealings with members of other cultures.

All this provides the basis for a rationality which is to be seen as necessarily involving a capacity for compromise on prejudgements in any situation where a clash of opinion occurs which will lead to unacceptable (to all parties) consequences if left unresolved or if 'resolved' by imposition by one party on the others. Consider the problem which arranged marriage poses for many young people descended from immigrants. Many young people find themselves suffering from a sort of 'schizophrenia' induced by the mismatch between the cultural values of their homes and those of the culture they participate in at school and in their other 'outside' activities.

Once we accept the provisional nature of our traditions' pre-judgements and the rationality of changing them in order to preserve a capacity to 'feel at home at home' we see that the important feature of this mismatch is not the (contingently) unanswerable question, 'who's right and who's wrong?', but the serious damage the failure to resolve this dis-agreement does to the psyches of many of the young people trapped in and being 'torn apart' by it.

My hope in proposing the approach under discussion is that once people see the pointlessness of blankly asserting the truth of their pre-ferred prejudgements they will see the rationality of compromising so as to maintain a society in which most people find it congenial to live. I can-not do more than hope since no understanding can guarantee that some-one will not cynically choose to pay lip service to a powerful culture (majority or, as in South Africa, minority) purely because that will facili-tate his or her achieving wealth and status. There is a problem of moral education here which is beyond the scope of this piece, but I would sug-gest that the examples of Northern Ireland and Sri Lanka indicate the irrationality of the belief that even a powerful majority can insulate itself adequately from manifestations of the resentment of a disgruntled minority. When the minority 'turns', everybody's quality of life suffers. Thus it seems to me that compromise in the interests of social stability is the rational course and that it is a respectable aim of education in schools to teach this.

Since the aim of this sort of conversation is not to reveal the 'TRUTH about the good life' but rather the achievement of a willing and workable compromise, it is not at all utopian, quite the opposite. The aim of com-promise involves trying to let as many people as possible keep as many of their prejudices as is possible under the constraint of keeping society via-ble as 'home' for all who live in it. This must obviously involve making sure that there is enough contact and mutual understanding so that racism by way of cross-cultural misinterpretation is minimized.

Through education for conversation as outlined, I believe we can teach the understanding and skills necessary for participation in such continuing and recurring conversation in ordinary, everyday life after school. A successful pluralism must be one in which such a conversation is established as customary practice. I am conscious, however, that the contribution of schools is unlikely to be sufficient on its own to establish the practice outlined here as customary. For that we need a wider educational approach and co-operation from mass media. How to implement these wider requirements is beyond my present brief, but the value of education for conversation in schools, guided by teachers sensitive to the issues and who are aware of likely disagreements and relevant cultural traditions, will be clear. Taking part in such a conversation would give pupils a valuable training in how to avoid fruitless conflict when they meet people with foundational prejudgements different from their own. It would inculcate personal skills in understanding others and discourage over-hastiness in judgement (particularly of the sort that leads to problems when we judge the behaviour of members of other cultures as if they were members of our own).

*   *   *

Much work remains to be done on how to conduct lessons designed to educate pupils in this art of conversation under the assumption of the universality of prejudice. And, of course, the approach I am recommending here is unlikely to work overnight. The time scale is likely to be long and changes undramatic. But we have too much evidence that legislation and militancy do little to eradicate racism. Perhaps now we must eschew the instant and dramatic solution and instead get on with the slow grind of education in an art which, if mastered to a reasonable degree, seems likely to discourage the slide from prejudice in favour of home to the dismissal out-of-hand of other culture's views and to racist practice. Having regarded prejudice as peripheral to human social being, tried to eradicate it and failed, I suggest we should now accept it as a central aspect of our being and get on with teaching ourselves how to cope with it.

Racial prejudice is very much a complementary phenomena to the fact that every true community is a community of both belief *and* sentiment. It results from a failure to acknowledge prejudice as prejudice and to cope with it rationally. My proposal is for an education that will correct this fundamental misunderstanding of tradition and our relation to it in a way that undermines the racist ideology and practice to which it often leads.

Notes

1. This account of prejudgement constitutes a modification of that given in my article 'Education and racism' (Jones, 1985). The changes incorporated here have been made largely because of responses made to a related paper read at the annual conference of the Philosophy of Education Society of Great Britain at the Froebel Institute College, 4-6 April 1986. (Jones, 1986). I am particularly indebted to Mr Victor Quinn, who replied to my conference paper and to Mr Derek Sankey who, in conversation after the formal session, pointed out the importance of traditional cosmologies.
2. Strawson 1977, p.9.
3. Ibid., p.10.
4. For a more complete account cf. Juan Mascaro's introduction to *The Upanishads*, 1977 particularly pp.11-15.
5. Parvez, 1968, is my source here, particularly pp.70-8.
6. This is not to suggest that economic considerations do not carry weight in Islamic politics. They do, but their influence is leavened by religious considerations to an extent which is not mirrored in modern European states.
7. On the tacit nature of our grasp of our native languages cf. Evans 1981, pp.118-37.
8. On the cultural diversity of conventions of interpersonal etiquette cf. Gumpertz, Jupp and Roberts, 1979.
9. For a more detailed discussion of these points see Jones, 1985.
10. Fromm, 1942.
11. Cf. Gumpertz et al., 1979.
12. Here I have been very much influenced by the work of Hans-Georg Gadamer, cf. Gadamer, 1981 — on prejudice pp.241-4, on conversation pp.330-1. More generally, my thoughts in this piece have been influenced by the article 'What is practice? The conditions of social reason' in Gadamer, 1983.

Racism, Self-esteem and the School
Patricia White

If self-esteem is dependent on the appraisal of others will not the prejudice of the dominant group enter into the stigmatized group member's perception of himself? (Davey, 1975, p.29. Quoted in Swann Report, 1985, p.47.)

What is self-esteem?[1] People with positive self-esteem have a favourable opinion of themselves. They see themselves, for instance, as having worthwhile ends in view and the necessary dispositions and capacities to pursue them; or as having achieved something worthwhile; or as the possessors of some desirable attribute, like good looks, talent, or as coming from a 'good family'. (If they have *high* self-esteem they have a *very* favourable opinion of themselves in these ways.) Those who have low self-esteem may see their ends as unworthy, or valueless, or they may be totally bewildered because there is no order to their life. They may, on the other hand, see themselves as, for example, too unintelligent, or too lacking in self-control to carry through a project, however worthy in conception it might be. They may have a poor opinion of themselves, too, because they feel they have accomplished little or nothing of any worth, or because they see themselves as personally unattractive or lacking in social status.[2]

Whether people are right in these positive and negative judgements is another matter. Someone who thinks he or she is unintelligent may be mistaken; and individuals are not perhaps the final authorities on the worthiness or unworthiness of their own ends. What matters for self-esteem — however high or low — is that one should *believe* that one is such and such. (I am not implying here that it is *all right* for one's self-esteem to be based on any beliefs whatsoever, including false ones. Nor am I implying that a high level of self-esteem can never be too high. More of this later.)

Much attention has been paid recently to students' self-esteem in schools. A reasonably high level of self-esteem is seen as important both

as a constituent part of personal well-being generally and as a prerequisite of educational achievement. A particular claim about students'
self-esteem which brings us back to the quotation at the head of this
paper is that the low achievement of many students from ethnic
minorities is due to their low self-esteem. This, in turn, it is often claimed,
is brought about to a large extent by racist prejudice directed towards
them by dominant groups, either personally or institutionally.[3]

This is a fiercely debated topic where research findings are frequently
contested and reinterpreted (see, e.g., Milner, 1983, ch.6 and pp.220-4). It
has been argued, for instance, that to link the under-achievement of
blacks in school with their alleged low self-esteem is to root the cause of
their failure in black children themselves, without being open to possible
causes in the education system (Stone, 1981).[4] It has also been suggested
that, despite what some studies would appear to show, there is no problem of low black self-esteem (ibid.). That of course is an empirical claim
and one which, it seems to me, is at least questionable, as the literature
indicates (for a review of some of the literature, see Milner, 1983,
ch.6).

In this chapter I do not want to go further into these debates. My main
concern is with what part schools can play in the area of self-esteem. I
shall argue that whether students have high or low self-esteem, educators
should be concerned that *all* their students come to experience their self-
esteem, and particularly its bases, as problematic and as a subject for far
reaching social and personal reflection. *If* my argument is sound,
however, and *if* the claim outlined above, about the causes and consequences of low self-esteem found among ethnic minority students, is correct, my proposals should help to increase the latter's self esteem and
make them less vulnerable to others' prejudices.

I

Before and since Swann, schools and other educational institutions
have both been trying to tackle their own institutional racism and such
examples of the wider racism in society as manifest themselves in
schools — graffiti and name-calling, for instance — as well as attempting
through the curriculum to examine the roots, ideology and practices of
racist prejudice. These efforts have often resulted, in part, in codes of

conduct and anti-racist statements.

How far might such measures help to enhance the low self-esteem of some students? Is it in this direction that we should look? The issue is an empirical one, but there is also a conceptual distinction which needs to be made in this area.[5] Self-esteem is sometimes confused with self-respect.[6] Self-respect is one's sense of one's dignity as a person. It is adversely affected when one's moral or political rights are impugned — if people treat one merely as a means to their own ends, for instance, wilfully break their promises to one, subject one to degradation, patronise one. People can have a lively sense of self-respect, their antennae quivering at any possible infringements of their rights, yet suffer from low self-esteem, believing, for instance, that nothing which they set out to accomplish could ever turn out well owing to their own inadequacies.

Coming back to schools' anti-racist guidelines, it is clear that these are supremely important for the self-respect of members of the school community, indeed the observing of them is essential to a moral community. They may, however, do little or nothing to enhance students' self-esteem.[7] I may think it right and proper that you do not abuse me by calling me names and I may even come to see myself as having a valuable contribution to make to the framing and implementation of the anti-racist policy of the school and yet I may at the same time have a low opinion of myself and my abilities in all other departments of school life.

II

Let us assume that a school in a racist society has done what it can to support the self-respect of its students, through anti-racist guidelines and the like. What can it do about its students' self-esteem?

There can be many discrete bases for positive self-esteem. By 'base' here I mean something, e.g., a practice, an activity, an achievement, a physical, mental or moral attribute, which one sees as worth pursuing or possessing. (In the same way, *mutatis mutandis*, there can be many bases for low self-esteem.) People may have equally high self-esteem but this may derive from different bases. The self-esteem of many people in Western societies is based on their occupational role — as solicitor, professor of psychology, master baker, Volvo worker — hence for many the trauma of retirement and now unemployment. (Here, as often elsewhere later in this chapter, I use 'self-esteem' as shorthand for 'positive self-esteem'. It should, I hope, be clear in each case from the context when I am doing this.) Others may derive their self-esteem as well, or instead, from other bases — being a good Muslim, steelband musician, being aggressively working-class and, even for some university teachers such are our contortions, being a middle-class simulacrum of a working-class person. (What a crass juxtaposition, it might be objected: how can one put 'being a good Muslim' alongside the other items in this list? Not to beg any questions at this point, however, I am not assuming that any one basis is 'better' than any other.) The possible bases for self-esteem are endless. We often mark this in a conversational way when trying to lift the spirits of friends: 'but look how good you are at getting people to work together'; 'but I would never have the patience to do that kind of work'; and, to women, 'but you have been a wonderful mother to those boys'. We cast around for one of the many alternative bases available.

This strategy of casting around for alternative bases for ourselves or others comes in part from trying to avoid the problem picked out by the quotation at the head of this chapter. Any of the bases I have mentioned can be radically affected by the views of fellow members of my community. I shall find it hard to derive my self-esteem solely from being an unskilled building labourer or 'only a housewife' in the United Kingdom in the 1980s since my esteem will be affected by the standing of those occupations in others' eyes. I can, as we have seen, move to other bases. Nozick, indeed, recommends, as a policy to communities who want to enhance the self-esteem of their members, increasing the number of dimensions on which people can measure themselves (Nozick, 1974. pp.245-6). Nielsen, whilst objecting to Nozick's taking over of bourgeois competitive values, reflected particularly in the competitive sports examples he chooses, similarly recommends increasing the dimensions by the inclusion of non-competitive activities such as, for instance, jogging and feeling your body come into better shape, or cross-country skiing (Nielsen, 1985, p.275). Leaving aside the question of whether Nielsen's suggestion works, the general strategy of increasing the dimensions on which people measure themselves is certainly one that schools employ in various subtle and not so subtle ways — not just prizes for academic work, but sports trophies, art exhibitions, displays of break dancing, the steel band: all these can be promoted as possible bases for self esteem. There are, though, serious difficulties in taking this path. Looked at from a prudential point of view, any basis can suffer the vagaries of changing public esteem. What *was* highly thought of is so no longer. So what happens to the self-esteem of the 'ordinary housewife' or the local bobby? They can move to other bases, but how to make the move without a loss of integrity? They can attempt to shore up the basis of their self-esteem and make it impregnable to public disregard or contempt. But how to do that?

Morally speaking, too, these bases for self-esteem have serious flaws. At their most innocuous they may lead to a stand-off, self-contained, stance to other people who are not policemen, steelband musicians or whatever; and at their worst to highly divisive, bigoted attitudes to others. *Self*-esteem is perhaps preserved but at the expense of an insulated attitude of indifference to the rest of one's community. In Western liberal societies, particularly in the 1980s under right-wing governments, it is possible to observe this phenomenon in a frighteningly fierce form. For self-preservation many people privatize the basis of their self-esteem and erect walls against the rest of society. Teachers often see these fiercer forms of self-esteem in members of minority groups and members of the majority population. In so far as they share the misgivings expressed here about the basis of this self-esteem they face a cruel moral dilemma. Should they attempt to destabilize the only basis for self-esteem this student has — being a loyal West Ham supporter, a Rastafarian, or seeing him or herself as having the attributes of a potential model? And, if so, in favour of what? What teacher will be so sure that he or she can offer a 'better' basis for self-esteem as to feel sanguine about venturing to dislodge a student from his or her preferred stance to the world? And if such teachers exist, would citizens and parents in a democratic community be happy to let them pursue their strategies of destabilization and substitution of values in the manner of a pedagogical CIA?

Yet even leaving aside, as I am doing in this discussion, morally reprehensible bases for self-esteem which would offend against the framework of any democratic society, e.g., membership of a Mafia gang, the pursuit of narrow, insulated kinds of self-esteem, as we have seen, involves dangers both for the individual and the quality of life in the whole community. Surely the educational institutions of any democratic society should try to counteract these? I think they must and I think that teachers can offer a quite different perspective on self-esteem, avoiding, at the same time, charges of manipulation and of sapping the confidence of their students. This perspective is, furthermore, very much in the spirit of the Swann Report and its underlying philosophy of education for all.

III

Schools, then, may well be uncertain about their students' chosen bases of self-esteem. At the same time they may not feel that they are in a position confidently to endorse some bases and (leaving aside the limited class of the reprehensible) condemn others and attempt to dislodge students from them. So what, as educational institutions, can they do? In the kind of democratic community the Swann Report has in mind educational institutions must, it seems to me, offer their students the chance openly and honestly to explore the bases of their (positive or negative) self-esteem. This exploration, which would have two aspects, would assume its full-bodied form in the secondary school, though the process could well be started in the first school.

On the one hand, (a), there would be the social, public aspect covering knowledge of the way society works and, how, in the broadest terms, one has become the person one is. This would be partly included in the political education outlined in Swann (pp.334-40), as well as in other relevant curriculum areas. It is crucially important for the individual's understanding of how he or she came to be the kind of person he or she is. We all, all too easily, fall prey to the myth of our total individual uniqueness which can be enormously damaging, if it leads us to think, e.g., that our neuroticism, fears, anxieties — as well indeed as our achievements and successes — are all uniquely our responsibility. No one who has any knowledge of the women's movement over the last few decades can have any doubt of the powerful effect of coming to understand how social forces help to shape individual lives. (A classic vignette is provided in Virginia Woolf's *A Room of One's Own*.) This kind of understanding is essential if one is to appreciate how it is, in general, that some social groups enjoy boundless self-esteem, whilst others do not. In this process history, the humanities and many aspects of the pastoral curriculum are of the first importance if students are to have an understanding of the social roots of their own and others' self-esteem. These are the last subjects a society endeavouring to raise the self-esteem of its citizens can afford to cut back on for the sake of efficiency and improved economic performance.

Schools should also not forget that they, as institutions, can structurally help to enhance or damage their members' self-esteem. It may be, for instance, that some activities in which members of minority groups do not participate on religious grounds are accorded high status in a school. In its exploration therefore, of differential social structural support for self-esteem the school should actively encourage its students to examine its own role in this process.

This public social knowledge and examination of both the wider and the more immediate structures in which individuals find themselves would be complemented, (b), by an exploration into the individual's own personal bases of (positive or negative) self-esteem. This will involve individuals in taking a 'stepping-back' (Smith, 1985, p.114ff.), reflective attitude to themselves and their bases of self-esteem as these have hitherto developed. Stepping back and considering your own personal bases of self-esteem is a process which will sometimes not be easy because of the painful honesty required. It will involve asking yourself whether, for you, some bases of self-esteem are more important than others and considering why this might be so. From what perspective are they more important? How justifiable is it to take that perspective? It is not an easy process but this effort at detachment from one's bases of self-esteem is something which education must encourage if students are not to be in the grip of feelings and attitudes which exert a powerful control over their lives, but which they have been neither equipped to understand nor enabled to modify. It might be argued that this is a process only for certain kinds of people, the naturally more reflective and articulate. But this is perhaps wrongly to assume that it depends on qualities which are not necessary to it. Gabriele Taylor (1985), following Charles Taylor (1985),[8] suggests that, for instance, reflection on one's desires may not depend on great articulateness:

> ... the 'articulation' may also consist in the person envisaging certain situations, or certain responses to a given situation, and then accepting or rejecting the picture so evoked: it may or may not 'feel right'. (G. Taylor, 1985, p.130)

Being helped, then, to take a reflective attitude to the roots of your self-esteem is one safeguard against being a victim of others' prejudices to which the quotation at the head of this chapter draws attention.

It is possible that this kind of second-order reflection may itself become a basis of positive self-esteem. It will be, in a sense, a self-esteem based on being, rather than doing, in that it will stem from the individual's attempts to bring his or her life into a certain kind of order. It does not preclude other more usual first-hand bases of self-esteem, but it puts these into a certain perspective so that the individual is not at their mercy. I am not saying, therefore, let me make it quite clear, that second-order self-esteem can *replace* the usual first-order sorts, deriving from the individual's athletic prowess, occupational skills, physical attributes, or whatever, and neither am I saying that there is necessarily anything wrong in a person's deriving satisfaction from such achievements or attributes. At the same time, however, there is much more of a general sort to be said about first order bases of self-esteem, including what constitutes an 'acceptable' level of self-esteem as well as a need for an exploration of the issues of relative values and priorities here. My only positive claim at this point is that, to avoid both personal and social harms (see section II above), first-order bases of self-esteem should be reflectively reviewed. I hope in future work both to pursue the value questions to do with first-order bases of self-esteem and to develop this second-order conception, considering further its possibility as a project for *all* students, its possible connections with self-respect and in what ways, if at all, it is assessable. I should like to show that it may be the most secure underpinning for anyone's self-esteem.[9]

It is perhaps appropriate at this point to stress that I would want to refute any claim that this suggestion for the enhancement of self-esteem is merely 'therapy', the latest prop to the status quo. Elsewhere I hope to develop a response to this objection, indicating how the reflective nature of this project offers some protection against manipulation both within and outside the educational institution, but here I will restrict myself to a brief comment. At the least, those engaging in this project will, on the social level, gain some insight into the need for transparency in a democratic society and some awareness of the ideological shields often raised by the powerful; whilst, on the personal level, they will achieve some awareness of the significance of the connections between honesty, self-deception and self-esteem. (For a philosophical discussion of this area, see G. Taylor, 1985, esp. chapter V). Both sorts of insights are essential prerequisites for any considered attempt to initiate changes in personal or social life.

Finally, encouraging individuals to develop a probing, reflective attitude to the bases of their self-esteem need not be, indeed should not be, seen as encouraging them in an individualistic and even narcissistic enterprise. If, as an educational institution, a school must help its members to achieve a detached and reflective attitude to their personal bases of self-esteem, there is every reason for this to be a collaborative matter to be achieved in a mutually supportive community. This is one educational policy which can unite the members of a pluralist society. It is true that first-order bases of self-esteem will differ and there always remains the possibility that they may conflict and produce antagonisms. Through this educational experience, however, students can be united in a common attempt at an honest exploration of the social and personal bases of their self esteem. In fact there is every reason for the exploration to take this form, if, as I indicated above, their education is to prepare students for the necessary processes of dealing with conflict and arriving at honourable compromises which, as other contributors have argued (see Haydon, Jones and John White), living in a pluralist society demands. In concrete institutional terms this conception of self-esteem offers considerable possibilities for unifying the pastoral curriculum around its twin foci of social and personal exploration. More than that, rather than being something organized *for* students, it should be the subject of a whole-school policy devoted to the encouragement and development of the self-esteem of all members of the school community. (For a related and highly relevant discussion, see Fielding, 1985.)

So conceived, the achievement of positive self-esteem and confidence is not the latest prize to be striven for in the academic competition ('my confidence profile is better than yours!') but an aim which can unite a whole educational community.

Notes

1. I should like to thank Professor Bhiku Parekh, and also, Paul H. Hirst and John White for helpful, constructive criticisms which have, I hope, led to a clearer expression of the main thesis of this paper.

2. In this brief account of self-esteem I am taking a rather broader view than John Rawls (1972, p.440) who sees self-esteem as having two aspects: 'it includes a person's sense of his own value, his secure conviction that his conception of his good, his plan of life is worth carrying out. And . . . implies a confidence in one's ability . . . to fulfil one's intentions.' It seems to me that a person's self-esteem can be rather less activity-oriented. He or she may take a favourable view of his or her worth because, e.g., he or she comes from a 'good family' or has 'good looks', neither of which need involve a project to be carried out. See also note 6 below.

3. As Swann tells us (Swann Report, 1985, ch.2, para.3.4 p.16) many teachers, for instance, have a scale of classroom acceptability with Chinese at the top and West Indians at the bottom.

4. The analysis I later offer is, I think, not open to this interpretation since it rejects an account of self-esteem explained wholly in terms of individual psychology.

5. For an illuminating discussion of the distinction between self-respect and self-esteem, see David Sachs' (1981) paper.
6. John Rawls (1972) in *A Theory of Justice* used the words 'self-respect' and 'self-esteem' interchangeably. Recently, however, Rawls (1985) has accepted, in a final footnote, that self-respect and self-esteem need to be distinguished.
7. R.E. Lane (1982) makes a similar point in relation to the enjoyment of political rights which Rawls (1972) had suggested would enhance self-esteem.
8. C. Taylor (1985), 'What is human agency?' in *Human Agency and Language*, Vol. 1.
9. It may be that it is possible, even desirable, for a person to experience neither positive nor negative self-esteem but that issue, too, and its possible implications I shall have to take up elsewhere.

'Education for All' and Religious Schools

T.H. McLaughlin

The Swann Report, *Education for All* (1985), despite some qualifications and reservations (ch.8, II, para.2.18), and a dissenting minority report (p.515), is opposed to, or is at least highly critical of, the concept of separate religious schools within the maintained system in England and Wales. Thus, whilst acknowledging the existing legal situation and the rights arising from it (ch.8, II, para 7.2), the report argues against the proposals made on religious and other grounds for the establishment of their own voluntary-aided schools by certain sections of the Asian, Muslim and Black communities (ch.8, II, paras 2 and 3). In addition, the report calls for a reconsideration of the existing dual system which provides for voluntary schools in general within the maintained sector (ch.8, II, para.2.19).[1]

This attitude to religious schools is likely to be, and has been, criticized and rejected by those who find themselves in fundamental disagreement with some of the central principles involved in Swann's conception of 'education for all' (see, for example, the Islamic Academy, 1985). It is also unlikely to appeal to those (for example, Haldane, 1986; Scruton et al., 1985) whose general perspective on a range of relevant issues is rather different from that of Swann.

In this chapter I do not intend to deal with the complex issues which arise from such conflicts of basic principle and value. For example, I shall not be concerned directly with a full analysis of the case for Muslim voluntary-aided schools, which requires an engagement with such fundamental conflicts, and with a range of other philosophical issues, which are beginning to receive sustained attention (Halstead, 1986). It is worth observing in passing, however, that in the light of arguments developed by some of my fellow contributors to this volume, the case against Muslim schools might appear to be less clear-cut than is often supposed. For example, a common charge against Muslim schools (expressed in its simplest form), is that they are likely to indoctrinate their pupils; to make insufficient provision for the development of their personal autonomy and their awareness of the demands of critical rationality. But in view of the claim of Graham Haydon, and others, that no one ethical theory or framework of values can be shown to be correct or true in any sense, what grounds might be appealed to in objecting to indoctrination, or in valuing the importance of personal autonomy, in the face of a self-consistent theory and framework which justifies different values?[2] And how confident can one be in asserting the importance of critical rationality in the light of the argument of Malcolm Jones about the scope of reason in human life and the limited role it can play in the evaluation of the foundational prejudgements or presuppositions of particular cultures or forms of life?

It may well be felt that views such as these, which at face value seem to undermine the foundations for some of the central principles implicit in *Education for All*, render more problematic an opposition to Muslim voluntary-aided schools.

Whether or not this is so, however, I shall be concerned in this chapter with more limited and specific questions about religious schooling which arise *within* the framework of these principles. If one accepts the essential features of Swann's conception of 'education for all', is one necessary committed to a rejection of religious schools? Are there at least some forms of religious schooling which could be compatible with these essential features, and, if so, what conditions must the aims and practices of such schools satisfy in order to achieve this compatibility? What motives could underlie support for such schools, and on what grounds might they be justified?[3]

In exploring these questions, I shall be accepting for the purposes of argument the central principles implied in Swann's conception of 'education for all', without examining questions about their justification. I shall also accept Swann's conception of the kind of society for which our educational system should be preparing all young people (ch.1). Although my discussion is in this sense 'internal' to the Swann Report, I shall not be confining my remarks to its detailed arguments, and shall be dealing with questions which go beyond its terms of reference. I therefore use the report as a framework within which I raise broader questions.

*   *   *

Since the term 'religious school' is ambiguous, it is appropriate for me to indicate clearly here how I intend to use it.

By 'religious school' in this discussion, I mean a school which (a) provides a full-time general education for its students; (b) in an institutional context in which the truth of a particular religion is presupposed and taught, and which seeks to develop in the students not just; (c) the understandings and commitments characteristic of the 'educated person', but also; (d) those of the 'religious person', where these include the development, to some extent and in some form, of a determinate religious commitment. To use the terminology employed in Swann, the school therefore seeks to undertake in the same institution the activities of 'education' and religious 'nurture' and 'instruction' (see ch.8, I, para.5.2).

In the light of (a), therefore, it is clear that I am not referring in this chapter to the various forms of 'supplementary' religious school which seek merely to provide an *addition* to the general education being received by the child elsewhere.

Like Swann, I shall confine myself to a consideration of the acceptability of religious schools within the maintained sector, and so shall be referring throughout to voluntary schools, although I have no space to explore in any detail issues relating to status and funding.

If we read Swann's view of what is implied in 'education' into (a) and (c), then precise questions which arise in relation to the compatibility of such schools with 'education for all' include the following: are (a) and (c) compatible (logically and empirically) with (b) and (d)? On what grounds, and with what justification, can it be claimed that (a), (b), (c) and (d) should be linked together in the same institution?

One might imagine that a good starting point for our discussion is the stance of the minority report (footnote p.515), whose rejection of Swann's position on religious schools was not based on a parallel rejection of its philosophy of 'education for all'. This, however, is of limited value for our purposes, because its defence of religious schools is confined to a claim about their contingent value and necessity until 'education for all' can be fully established. Thus, the minority statement concedes that 'If and when Education for All is a reality, there will be no need for separate schools' (ibid.). There is no attempt to consider and develop an argument to the effect that, even when fully implemented, the character of the principles of 'education for all' are such that they are compatible with a legitimate plurality in forms of schooling; a plurality which licenses certain forms of religious school.

*   *   *

I have no space here to attempt a detailed analysis of all the principles
involved in 'education for all', and to trace the different kinds of principle, their relationship to each other and the contradictions and tensions
between them.[4] In this section, I intend simply to outline four principles
which seem to me to be not only fundamental to the concept of 'education for all', but also most clearly at odds with the notion of a religious
school. For convenience, I will refer to these principles as the 'personal
autonomy', the 'breadth and diversity of curriculum', the 'differentiation
of responsibilities' and the 'opposition to separate provision'
principles respectively.

(i) The 'personal autonomy' principle
Swann is clearly committed in a fundamental way to the value of a principle which might be roughly expressed as the freedom of the individual
as a rationally autonomous agent in a pluralist, democratic society.
Although for convenience I shall refer to this principle as one involving
'personal autonomy', it is important to note that this is not intended to
overlook the important point that, for Swann, the kind of agency that is
being aimed at is one that is to be exercised within the context of a particular conception of society (ch.1), a conception which has important
implications for the character of the autonomous agency in question.
Throughout this chapter I am therefore using the term 'personal
autonomy' in a specific sense which includes this important condition.
Coupled to this conception is a view of education which has as one of its
central aims the development of such persons. Elements of this commitment can be seen throughout the report. For example, it insists that 'It is
important to emphasise . . . free choice for individuals, so that all may
move and develop as they wish within the structure of the pluralist
society' (ch.1, para.4), and argues that, in schools, 'All pupils should be
given the knowledge and skills needed . . . to determine their own
individual identities, free from preconceived or imposed stereotypes . . .'
(ch.6, para.1.4). Schools must therefore avoid imposing a 'predetermined
and rigid' cultural identity on any student so as to restrict their freedom
to 'decide as far as possible for themselves their own future way of life'
(ch.6, para.2,5). With regard to matters of schooling and religion, a major
aim of religious education should be to enable students to ' . . . determine
(and justify) their own religious position' (ch.8, I, para 2.11).

(ii) *The 'breadth and diversity of curriculum' principle*
As a consequence of the educational implications of (i), and as part of what is involved more generally in education for a pluralist, democratic society, Swann insists that all pupils be exposed in a systematic and appropriately objective way to a broad range of values, beliefs, ways of life and life ideals. Thus '. . . a good education must reflect the diversity of British Society and . . . the contemporary world' (ch.6, para.2.1), and the curriculum for all pupils '. . . must be permeated by a genuinely pluralist perspective which should inform and influence both the selection of content and the teaching materials used' (ch.6, para.3.1). In the area of religion, too, pupils must be given the opportunity 'to enhance their understanding of a variety of religious beliefs and practices' (ch.8, I, para.1.2).

(iii) *The 'differentiation of responsibilities' principle*
Swann characterizes in a very clear way the respective responsibilities of the school and the home/religious community with regard to religion. In general for Swann, the school does not have a responsibility for the *reinforcement* or *preservation* of the values, beliefs and cultural identities of pupils. The task of the school is appropriately to *develop* these (ch.6, para.2.5), in the light, for example, of principles (i) and (ii) above. Applied specifically to religion, this principle holds that schools do not have a responsibility for 'nurturing' 'instructing' or 'maintaining' religious beliefs and practices. These tasks are the prerogative of the home (if it wishes to undertake them), and the religious community, and may include 'community-based provisions for religious instruction' (ch.8, I, para.5.2) complementary to the work of the school. The responsibility of the school as seen by Swann is the educational one of assisting its students 'to understand the nature of religion and to know something of the diversity of belief systems, their significance for individuals, and how these bear upon the community' (ch.8, I, para.2.8).

(iv) *The 'opposition to separate provision' principle.*
In a quite general way, Swann stresses its 'fundamental opposition' to any form of 'separate provision' (see, for example, ch.7, para.2.10), and stresses the need for '. . . *all* pupils to share a common educational experience which will prepare them for life in a truly pluralist society' (ch.8, II, para.2.11).

*   *   *

At first sight, the task of reconciling principles (i) - (iv) with the notion of a religious school would seem to be a difficult one. Is not each of them straightforwardly in conflict with such a notion?

I shall seek to show, however, that when the complexity of the principles and their implications is examined, it is possible to see how scope exists for the development of an argument to the effect that at least certain kinds of religious school can be seen as compatible with the essential ideas contained in each principle. This argument can only be sketched briefly here. While I shall attempt in due course to indicate some of the difficulties that the argument faces in order to become fully plausible, a full treatment of all these matters is beyond the scope of this chapter. I nevertheless hope that the discussion will be useful in drawing attention to arguments which may be worthy of fuller development and assessment.

I shall consider each of the four principles in turn. The kind of religious school that might be compatible with 'education for all' will emerge progressively throughout the discussion.

(i) *The 'personal autonomy' principle*
If we accept that a principle of this form can be justified as an aim of education when stated in an appropriately nuanced way in the face of recent critiques (see, for example, Dunlop, 1986; Godfrey, 1984; Lloyd, 1981; Ward, 1983; White, J. 1984a), it remains an open question what conditions — especially conditions of schooling — actually help to facilitate and develop the aim. It is not clear that the kind of common school envisaged by Swann, even granted its successful implementation, is necessarily the *only* way in which this is best promoted.

One rather crude way of developing this point is to refer to the fact that many people seem to achieve an independence of mind about religious issues despite having received what appears to be a very restrictive and determinate form of religious schooling and training (see, for example, Kenny, 1986).[5] But this observation cannot licence *any* form of religious schooling. The element of risk and randomness has to be taken into consideration. Any religious school compatible with the principle of the development of autonomous agency must be able to show that it is, in virtue of its aims and practices, *likely* to develop such agency in its students, albeit in a distinctive way.

In what follows, I shall try to develop the idea that *one* way in which autonomy might be developed is *from the basis of* a form of schooling *within* a determinate religious tradition of belief, value and practice. A fuller outline of what I have in mind here will emerge in subsequent discussion. Such a schooling seeks not to *confine* its pupils within the tradition, but to use it as a substantial basis from which pupils might be launched on their own search for autonomous agency. Religious schools engaged in such a task can, I suggest, be seen as fulfilling this first principle of 'education for all' in a distinctive way, and can be regarded as a legitimate alternative to the common schools favoured by Swann. Both kinds of school can be seen as having their advantages and disadvantages in this respect and neither can be seen as having privileged status.

A general point about any educational conditions which are likely to favour the development of autonomy is that they must establish a balance between two sets of demands. I shall characterize these demands very roughly as 'openness' and 'stability' respectively. By 'openness' I refer to those features of a child's education which enable them to avoid being trapped in the possible limitations of the 'present and particular' (Bailey, 1984). Included here is an emphasis upon critical questioning; a broad knowledge of the variety and legitimate diversity of belief, practice and value; the importance of a person's making judgements and commitments about belief and action on the basis of evidence and grounds which they have assessed in the light of reason; the dangers of making unduly determinate commitments in the face of objective uncertainty, and so on. In contrast, 'stability' refers to the significance of, and need for, 'the present and the particular', if children are not to be disorientated and to lack a context for the development of their intellectual, moral, emotional and practical lives. Here there is an emphasis upon the limits of critical questioning; knowledge of, and adherence to, a substantiality of belief, practice and value; the significance of authorities and the wisdom contained in traditions; the difficulties involved in establishing merely formal criteria of evaluation for belief and value, and so on.

What seems clear is that some appropriate *balance* needs to be struck between these two broad demands in any adequate characterization of the kinds of educational conditions likely to develop personal autonomy. But where should this balance be struck? Is the kind of religious school I have sketched one which might embody an acceptable balance, or can such a balance only be found within the parameters of the common school?

It is important to note that this question cannot be answered satisfactorily in the abstract, or on philosophical grounds alone. A wide range of complex empirical judgements about the operation of particular institutions in particular contexts would be required, for example, as part of any full treatment of the question. Granted that there is no incoherence in any aspect of the proposal, it would seem that *in principle* certain forms of religious schooling might satisfy (i).

This possibility, together with some of the arguments which might be used in favour of the kind of religious schools I characterize, emerges inadvertently from the positions taken by some of my fellow contributors. They acknowledge the significance and importance of aspects of 'stability', and are conscious of the dangers arising from a neglect of them. John White, for example, outlines the connection between the possession of a hierarchy of values and a person's sense of their self-identity, which can be threatened by any 'acute incoherence' in these values, arising, for example, from the 'Babel of values' in the broader society (p.16 above). Patricia White draws attention to the fragility of a person's self-esteem arising from the fact that the basis of it may be dependent upon the changing perceptions and valuations of others in the community (p.57ff. above). Malcolm Jones, as part of a considerable emphasis upon the importance of tradition, brings out the significant effects of becoming alienated from the 'modes of judgement and practice' in which we have been brought up: a person can be in conflict with the habits of feeling and response acquired in their early socialization and their conscious decisions at odds with their deepest tacit beliefs. The result of this, according to Jones, may be 'confusion, loss of assuredness and self-doubt' (p.49 above). Graham Haydon acknowledges the inadequacy of the abstract individualism of the liberal tradition of political philosophy and brings out how any adequate resolution of the questions he addresses must acknowledge the 'rootedness' of persons in diverse traditions or blends of them (p.27ff. above).

In other work, John White (1984b) stresses the significance of settled conventions for the task of educating the emotions, and Malcolm Jones (1986) criticizes Swann for failing to take account of the need to establish pupils in 'reflective awareness' of their cultural identities, a prerequisite of the self-awareness, critical capacity and emotional security necessary for participation in 'cross-cultural negotiation'.[6]

One reaction to these points is to call for a form of schooling which satisfies them by simply confirming and maintaining its students in a particular religious or cultural tradition. But this would fail to do justice to the demands of 'openness', and would clearly fall foul of Swann's fundamental principles. My concern here is merely to explore whether there can be different kinds of appropriate balance between the demands of 'stability' and 'openness' in 'schools', such that the common school can be seen as not necessarily the *only* context in which it can be achieved.

An obvious worry, for example, is whether the common school can adequately meet these various demands of 'stability'. Might not self-identity, self-esteem, psychic and emotional unity, moral development, critical capacity, emotional security and so on be threatened by too high a level of 'openness' (in its various aspects) in the common school; by a 'Babel of values' at school level? Is it not arguably the case that the greater degree of interim coherent stability in the religious school might not better facilitate the development of the autonomy of its pupils? Might it not have other advantages, too, for example, in counterbalancing for pupils prevailing and dominant conceptions and prejudices in society?

In defence of the common school it may well be urged that the dangers arising from 'openness' have been exaggerated. Although the concerns expressed can only be fully resolved in the light of empirical enquiry, such schools, it will be claimed, operate according to a very clear set of *principles* concerning reason, knowledge, values and the like which yield a defensible, practical and balanced view of all the aspects of 'openness' — and enable them to be appropriately related to those of stability (see, for example, Hirst, P.H., 1985; Crittenden, 1982). A set of firm principles is available to underpin the work of the common school and assist it in resolving the two sets of demands in an adequate way.

Reflection upon some of the arguments of my fellow contributors might lead us not to accept this defence too uncritically, for some of their arguments seem to undermine foundations upon which such principles have been based. Thus we discover that we lack both an agreed framework of common values in our society, and an idea of what such a framework should include; that we can identify no independently justified ethical theory which would provide us with a set of fundamental moral principles which we could use to settle particular issues; that reason has only limited scope in dealing with these matters, and so on. Such claims might lead us to think that the confident claims of the previous paragraph are less secure than they appear, and that the dangers arising from 'openness' in the common school are real. This worry is not

merely, then, one about the contingent shortcomings of particular common schools, but about whether a firm and coherent set of principles can
be outlined to govern their work and to give some indication about how
the 'balance' in question might be struck. John White alludes to the difficulties here when he refers to the 'ethical dilemmas' facing teachers
who have to bring up children within a defensible and coherent scheme
of values when we as yet have no clear collective agreement about what
that scheme should consist of.[7]

The force of these worries about the stability of the common school
would seem to be borne out by Graham Haydon's proposal that the
rather open-ended negotiation of values that he calls for — in which
even the ground-rules for the debate are themselves open to negotiation
— be conducted at *school level* (p.33 above).

What emerges from this is the need for a much fuller account to be
given of how the common school, in both theory and practice, might
meet this range of concerns before it can be accepted as the only, or best,
way of developing personal autonomy for all students.

The case for the kind of religious school I have sketched is
strengthened by considerations relating to the character of religion and
religious understanding. A major consideration here concerns the
significance of involvement in and with a particular religious tradition
for the ability to understand and evaluate it, and to work out one's own
position in relation to it. The 'phenomenological' approach to religious
education recommended by Swann has its disadvantages in this respect.
The approach through involvement, of course, has its own disadvantages. Might it not be claimed, however, that these are two *alternative*
bases from which a school might work in developing the autonomy of its
students in the area of religion?

Religion is not mentioned in any detail by any of my fellow contributors. It is not clear whether it is envisaged that religion should be one
of the issues included in the processes of negotiation, compromise and
conversation, since these are confined to issues of communal
significance. It does seem clear, however, that such processes — particularly if conducted at school level — are not very suitable for religious
questions, not least because of their substitution of 'practical compromise' for a search for truth. John White is surely correct in claiming
that, given this treatment, religious values would eventually disappear
(p.22 above).

What has emerged from this section, therefore, is a claim that a certain kind of religious school might constitute an alternative to the common school in providing a set of educational conditions likely to develop the autonomy of young people. Such a school provides through its particular religious tradition a context of relative stability of belief, practice and value, with the aim, not of entrapping pupils within it, but of providing them with a base from which their self-determination can proceed.

Such a school would, of course, have to satisfy certain conditions if it were to be acceptable for this role. For example, it would have to include a clear commitment to the development of autonomy as part of its aims, and be able to show that its practices were consistent with this aim. The character of these required conditions will emerge in subsequent discussion.

(ii) *The 'breadth and diversity of curriculum' principle*
How might the kind of religious school I have sketched in the last section deal with the requirement for breadth and diversity of curriculum? Even though such a school might have the aspiration of leading its pupils towards autonomy, is it not the case that the attention and commitment of its students are being focused upon the determinate beliefs and practices of just one religion? I think that such a school might meet this challenge in two ways. First, in relation to the religious aspects of its work, the school should ensure that it is not simply providing religious nurture, but a form of nurture which is capable of acting as a basis for the kind of open, phenomenological approach to religion which Swann recommends. Thus such a school would not eschew the phenomenological approach and the breadth and diversity associated with it, but would introduce it to its pupils at an appropriate point as part of its efforts to develop their autonomy in religion *from* the basis of a particular religious tradition.

Second, in relation to its general curriculum provision, the school should offer a broad curriculum which satisfies all the conditions of breadth and diversity stipulated in *Education for All*, and which is equally committed to preparing pupils for life in a pluralist, democratic society. This implies that whilst the general curriculum of the religious school might have a particular flavour or series of emphases, it must not be domesticated to religious ends; the various disciplines, for example, must be fully independent (for a related discussion see Walsh, 1983).

(iii) *The 'differentiation of responsibilities' principle*
It would seem that such schools clearly fall foul of this principle, since in offering a form of religious nurture they attempt a function which is clearly seen by Swann as the sole responsibility of the home and religious community.

This principle needs, however, to be stated in a more sophisticated way in the light of our earlier discussion. Religious schools of the sort we have been discussing are compatible with certain fundamental points that the principle seeks to capture — namely that the common school has no mandate to engage in any form of religious nurture, and that parents and the religious community have responsibility for any that is provided for the child.

But what Swann does not consider is the possibility of 'nurture' and 'education' being brought into a more complex relationship of the sort briefly sketched earlier. If this is admitted, then the distinctions upon which this principle depends (for example, that between 'maintaining' and 'developing' beliefs), and which are used to identify and allocate the 'differential responsibilities', need to be made in a more subtle way. The possibility is opened up of parents and the religious community exercising their right to provide a religious formation in the context of a form of schooling which links it with their child's education.

What motives might parents have in seeking this form of schooling for their children? To be compatible with the principles of Swann these motives must satisfy certain conditions, i.e. parents must value for their children the kind of autonomous agency characterized in (i); must not be motivated by racist considerations; must be genuinely committed to the educational aspects of their child's schooling; and so on. But within this framework of assumptions, several motives compatible with Swann's principles might be discerned. Parents might be concerned, for example, to ensure that their child's religious formation is not limited, narrow and divorced from its wider educational experience, as it conceivably might be if left solely to the family and the religious community. Further, parents may claim that in giving their child a clear, initial, non-restrictive identity, they are giving them a very important foundation for their life in a pluralist, democratic society, and making a contribution to that society itself.

Another aspect of this question concerns parents' rights, which is a subject which Swann does not deal with in other than a legal sense. Swann calls into question the legal rights that parents and communities currently enjoy concerning the establishment of voluntary schools. It might be felt by some that, in the light of *Education for All*, such parents do not have a moral right to establish such schools. But whilst the principles of 'education for all' cannot be rendered compatible with an acknowledgement of *unlimited* parental moral rights over the education of their children, parents may see the availability of certain forms of religious schooling as an extension of their moral rights to provide their children with a distinctive 'primary culture', which does not infringe the demands of autonomy, but provides a distinctive basis for it (McLaughlin 1984, 1985; Callan, 1985). Recognition of such a moral right is arguably compatible with Swann's basic educational principles. This observation should be borne in mind in any reconsideration of the legal rights which currently exist.

(iv) *The 'opposition to separate provision' principle*
Since a fundamental opposition to separate provision of any kind seems to be *built into* the concept of 'education for all', how can religious schools of however liberal a character be regarded as compatible with it?

One can question, however, just how *fundamental* this principle is in fact to 'education for all'. As is well known, Swann does in fact provide, on various grounds, separate provision in the case of single-sex schooling (ch.8 II, para.2.15). Why is *gender* rather than, say, *religion* being singled out as an acceptable criterion of separation?

The answer which Swann might give to this is that in such schools the *general character* of the education that is being provided is no different from that in mixed schools operating on the principle of 'education for all': it is not a special kind of education with different aims and content (of the sort that might be offered in a Muslim girls' school, for example). The variable involved in this instance of separate provision might be claimed therefore not to be a significant one (for critical comment on this, see Taylor, M.J., 1986).

What this seems to reveal is that there are at least two senses of the term 'separate provision' implicit in Swann. In the strong sense, 'separate provision' refers to provision which not only creates separate or distinct groups of students, but also seeks to achieve with them kinds of objectives that are very much at odds with the principles of 'education for all' (see ch.8, II, para.2.16). In the 'weaker sense', 'separate provision' refers simply to the creation for various reasons of separate or distinct groups of students whose schooling does not infringe these principles in any significant sense, but seeks to satisfy them in a particular way.

Since Swann seems to allow 'separate provision' in the weaker sense in the case of single-sex schooling, it is difficult to see how there can be objection to the kind of religious school I have been characterizing, which, if my earlier arguments are accepted, can be seen, parallel to single-sex schools, as institutions which are not in conflict with the fundamental principles of 'education for all', but seek to achieve these in a distinctive context.

*   *   *

In this final section I shall try to outline some of the critical questions which arise concerning the argument sketched in this chapter, and the conception of religious schooling involved in it. These — and other — questions require further detailed exploration before a final judgement can be made about the overall plausibility of the argument.

With regard to (i), the 'personal autonomy' principle, a critical question arises concerning the suggestion that the religious school is aiming to provide in the same institution *both* a form of (determinate) religious nurture *and* education (as Swann understands that term). Paul H. Hirst holds that these two kinds of activity are logically different from each other, in that they have (for example) fundamentally different aims. Further, whilst the two sets of activity may be mutually *compatible*, any institution attempting to undertake *both* in the same context must ensure that they are very sharply distinguished from each other not only in the minds of teachers, but also in the institutional policies and practices of the school. It is only in this way, claims Hirst, that such a school can avoid creating misunderstanding and confusion (Hirst, P.H., 1981). To meet these points, our suggestion that a form of religious nurture might constitute a substantial basis from which a child's education might proceed would require further detailed analysis and defence. It would be necessary, for example, to determine the precise relationship that is envisaged between the elements of 'education' and 'nurture' and to defend that relationship in the light of important distinctions that must be preserved. Further, an outline of implications for the practices and life of the school is required which do not result in its having, as Hirst would seem to recommend, the kind of fragmented and disjointed character that was identified as a danger of the common school.

Another difficulty is that, even granted the benefits of a child's education being conducted in relation to a particular tradition of belief, practice and value, further defence is required of the view that a *religious* tradition should be allowed to have so much salience in a child's schooling.

Several difficulties arise from the side of religion. First, can all religious faiths accommodate the kind of commitment to personal autonomy that is envisaged in this argument? It would seem that at least some faiths would be resistant to such an accommodation. If this is so, might it not be claimed that, to avoid the invidious and highly controversial task of distinguishing religious faiths capable of establishing acceptable voluntary schools from those that are not, as a matter of public policy no voluntary schools should be supported? Second, and more generally, what exactly is the character and force of the claim made about the significance of involvement and practice for a capacity to understand a religion, in contrast to the kind of understanding that can be gained from the 'phenomenological' approach to religious education?

Several of the concerns about the coherence of the relationship between the 'nurturing' and 'educating' functions of the religious school emerge specifically in relation to (ii), the 'breadth and diversity of curriculum' principle. How, for example, is the religious teaching offered from the standpoint of 'nurture' to be related to that offered from a 'phenomenological' perspective? How can the potential conflict between the two be resolved, and the differences between them marked out? A further problem arises from the insistence that the general curriculum of the school be largely independent from determination by religious considerations. In the light of this, what force has the claim that a *separate school*, rather than, say, the provision of supplementary religious schooling, is necessary for the pupils in question? If an answer to this is given in terms of the effects of the committed ethos of the school, then what implications does this have for the demands of breadth and diversity?

Since my argument in relation to (iii), the 'differentiation of responsibilities' principle, depends upon claims to which I have already indicated some critical objections, I shall proceed to an outline of the difficulties that arise concerning (iv), the 'opposition to separate provision' principle. Here it may be felt that insufficient justice has been done to

Swann's concerns about separate provision. What, for example, about the danger of religious schools leading to social divisiveness and attitudes related to it (see, for example, ch.8, II, paras. 2.12, 2.14)? Whilst it should be noted that such claims wait upon empirical support (Haldane, 1986), and that there are complexities in assuming that a straightforward connection exists between the development of tolerance and attendance at common, as distinct from, religious schools (Thiessen, 1986), it may still be felt that there is a *prima facie* case to answer here. One needs also to consider the various educational arguments against separation, involving claims about the educational significance of pupils mixing together throughout their schooling, encountering a variety of views from particular persons rather than from hypothetical or abstract sources, and receiving their education in a school which is thereby forced to make 'education for all' a reality.

There is a need, therefore, for an examination of the adequacy of the various steps that religious schools might take to overcome these criticisms: for example, by broadening the character of their intake to include a certain proportion of students who are not adherents of the particular religion in question; by demonstrating that they can make a distinctive contribution to social justice and harmony, and so on.

A further general concern about my argument might be that it alludes insufficiently to the specific issues which were the concern of Swann, namely those arising in relation to the education of children from ethnic minority groups. Given that particular context, it might be claimed, many of the arguments against separate religious schools take on a much more forceful and urgent significance.

*   *   *

This chapter has examined only a limited question in relation to religious schooling: whether some kinds of religious school are compatible with the principles of Swann's 'education for all'.

In view of all the complexities involved in this suggestion, the issues requiring further exploration and the critical challenges that need to be met, I consider that this question is an open one which is worthy of fuller investigation.

It should be noted, however, that establishing whether such schools can be compatible with the principles of 'education for all' is only a part of developing a full case that they should be accepted as part of the maintained school system of England and Wales. A judgement about this broader matter requires a full consideration of all the relevant practical, legal, demographic, political, etc., issues and implications, together with an assessment of the attitudes and requirements of the various religious communities.

It may be that the case for separate religious schools must be made independently of, and in opposition to, the principles of 'education for all'. I hope to have shown that, at least in the case of certain kinds of religious school, that conclusion should not be drawn too hastily.

Notes

1. Ann Dummett, a member of the Swann Committee for part of the inquiry, claims that the call in the report for a reconsideration of the whole position of voluntary schools is a cautious way of saying that they should be abolished (Dummett 1986, p.13). It should be noted, however, that Swann is careful not to express a view on this matter, which lies outside its terms of reference.
2. This question is in fact directly posed by Haydon in another article. See Haydon, 1986, p.99.
3. In this chapter I shall confine myself to a consideration of separate religious schools, and shall not consider any of the other important grounds on which separate schools might be sought.
4. For further discussion of some of these issues see Taylor, 1986.
5. It should not, of course, be assumed that a person who has achieved independence of mind about religious issues is necessarily one who has rejected religious faith.
6. See also John and Patricia White, 1986.
7. For a discussion of the significance for religious schools of disagreement and relativism see Aspin, 1983.

Affirmative Action and Positive Discrimination

Stuart Devall

The Swann Committee's history of work in progress is unusually controversial: rumours of internal divisions of opinion, Mr Arthur Rampton's dismissal by the Secretary of State, Mr Mark Carlisle, and Lord Swann's appointment, further rumours, the re-writing of a chapter on achievement, accusations and committee member resignations — all led to much speculation and anticipation. By contrast, an impression of uncharacteristic harmony seemed to be reflected in the report's reception; the media, professional bodies, educationalists and other academics and interested parties appeared impressed by its lengthy and appropriately detailed analysis (and even united in their attempts at witty allusions to the Swann of Marcel Proust's novel).

The recommendations of the report, however, have received a varied response. Some have claimed that, where they are not equivocal or too concerned with bureaucratic appointments and statements of mere intention, they are too few and too cautious to provide clear, adequate guidance, and to generate the changes that are necessary to create the 'education for all' that is the avowed aim. On the other (and more influential) hand, so far as policy implementation is concerned, Sir Keith Joseph clearly found some of the recommendations to be unacceptable and, seeing no need to justify his action, promptly rejected them. He was, of course, entitled to his opinion. He was also uniquely placed to exercise it in practice and, given the absence of self-evident truths in such complex issues, it is difficult to comprehend why he did not present a full explanation of the reasons for his action when his beliefs were in conflict with the conclusions drawn after such protracted, detailed research and deliberation.

For all its considerable explanatory length, some of the report's conclusions are curious, if not inconsistent. Rightly or wrongly, our society accepts the existence of Church of England, Roman Catholic, Jewish and other religious schools, so why should the establishment of other, separate, religious schools be regarded as being undesirable and avoid-able? If the existence of Muslim schools is divisive and contrary in theory and practice to the concept of 'education for all', why should the same not apply to all schools which use admission criteria of religion (and, perhaps, status or wealth)? Do they not also run contrary to the general aim of 'ideological cultural pluralism' and, in respect of denominational schools, to the 'broader phenomenological approach to religious educa-tion' that the report favours?

An equally strange conclusion is the rejection of bilingual teaching in schools. The report draws attention to the fact that 'some ethnic minority pupils . . . have particular language needs, either because English is not their first language or because they speak a dialect of English which dif-fers from the Standard English of the school' (Swann Report, 1985, ch.6, para.2.9), and affirms, 'our aim is to accord ethnic minority pupils equality of access and opportunity in a society in which a full command of Standard English is and will remain a key factor in success both in academic terms and in adult life' (ibid.). This aim seems uncontentious, but it is far from clear why bilingual teaching should not be regarded as a legitimate means of achieving it. Few would claim that the quality and extent of English as a second language provision in maintained schools have been sufficient to meet the needs in full, yet the report fails to evaluate the efficacy of relevant policies practised elsewhere. It is, at least, worthy of consideration that the United States, for example, has a well-established policy of enforcing the legal right of ethnic minority children (where nine or more of a particular group attend a school) to be taught in their first language during a one or two year transitional period. Such a measure, if adopted here, would seem fully compatible with fos-tering 'an understanding of the shared values of our society as a whole, as well as to an appreciation of the diversity of lifestyles and cultural, religious and linguistic backgrounds which make up this society and the wider world' (ch.6, para. 1.4), as well as with providing the knowledge and skills needed 'to determine their own individual identities' (ibid.). It would also have the effect of ensuring the appointment of specialist staff who would not be ignorant of the very languages that would facilitate the acquisition of a full command of Standard English. Separate schools for such purposes would be neither desirable nor necessary; from the outset only a proportion of the children's lessons would be taught in their first language, determined according to perceived needs — and, as these needs diminished, the proportion would be reduced. As the practice would be designed to supplement and increase the efficiency of ESL teaching and not to replace it, it is difficult to see why the report did not give it fuller consideration.

A possible but unstated contributory reason for the rejection might arise from a desire to avoid controversy concerning staff appointments — a clouded and confused area where misunderstanding and hostility are commonplace. My intention is to attempt to clarify two very distinct aspects of such appointments that are often conflated, yet which invoke very different considerations.

*   *   *

First, if a bilingual teaching policy were implemented, a clear consequence would be an expansion in the training and appointment of ethnic minority language teachers. Even under existing ESL arrangements fluency in a relevant ethnic language is a highly valuable asset which should be utilized more fully in specialist teacher training, and used as a legitimate criterion in appointments. The relevant criterion is *bilingualism*, not race or ethnicity, and, in so far as ability were assessed fairly in that respect, there would seem to be no cause for complaint from any quarter, though the probable consequence would be an increase in the number of ethnic minority teachers.

A related and equally compelling case arises in the area of pastoral care. In the opening chapter the report stresses the importance of membership of a particular *ethnic* group as 'one of the most important aspects of an individual's identity — in how he or she perceives him or herself and in how he or she is perceived by others' (ch.1, para.2). It is acknowledged that widely different ethnic traditions are an asset to our society, yet, even with the best of will, it is often very difficult, if not impossible, for someone outside a particular ethnic tradition to comprehend fully the different cultural and family-related beliefs and practices that have such a profound effect on children's development. Nevertheless, familiarity with and a sympathetic understanding of those influences, combined with an ability to provide guidance and practical assistance to children in need, are criteria for appointment and not a candidate's race or ethnic origin: pastoral appointments, particularly in urban areas with a large number of ethnic minority children, might *appear* to favour teachers from similar ethnic groups, but under our present laws it is illegal to discriminate on such grounds — and there is no substantial evidence that it is done: in fact, the low proportion of ethnic minority teachers is a major area of concern in the Swann Report.

Secondly, the above cases must be clearly differentiated from the concept of 'positive discrimination', which entails the distinguishing of a specific group or groups within a society, and devising and implementing special policies which favour those groups in comparison with other members of society — thereby being distinct from discrimination between people (which entails drawing a distinction, but does not necessitate further action) and negative discrimination (which restricts, or denies to some people, the resources, opportunities, or benefits enjoyed by others). The report states that ethnic minority teachers are still subject to racial prejudice and (negative) discrimination, both in gaining employment and in advancing their careers, and urges the Commission for Racial Equality and those responsible for making appointments to devote far greater efforts to identifying and overcoming racist obstacles to employing and promoting ethnic minority teachers. But it summarily dismisses the idea of positive discrimination in the form of quotas and fails to consider alternative forms.

Given the major obstacles experienced by ethnic minority teachers, and the report's expressed concern for the 'fundamental values such as a belief in justice and equality' (ch.1, para.2) and desire to promote 'an appreciation and commitment to the principles of equality and justice' (ch.6, para.2.3), it is odd that the case for positive discrimination was not examined in greater detail. Ability to rectify negative discrimination is dependent upon a thorough understanding of its scale, and it is for this reason that the interim report recommended that ethnically based statistics should be collected on pupils, teachers and student teachers. Sir Keith Joseph as Education Secretary failed to ensure that the recommendation was implemented and, in suggesting that eventually 'local authorities can operate acceptable and mutually compatible schemes which respect confidentiality' (*Guardian* 15 March 1985), implied the exclusion both of a national scheme, and freedom of information in respect of any statistics that may be collected. The probable consequence of such diluted measures is that disparate policies and confidentiality (or secrecy) will ensure that the present state of affairs will not be rectified. Public ignorance will be guaranteed.

If, as I would claim, a uniform system for compiling ethnically based statistics which are made available to the public is a prerequisite for rectifying negative discrimination, it is clearly not sufficient — and it is here that the Swann Report reveals one of its critical weaknesses — merely to urge greater efforts in identifying and overcoming racist obstacles to employing and promoting ethnic minority teachers. The report fails to recommend a policy with the teeth which will ensure that indifference, lethargy, or even hostility to the removal of these obstacles, are not permitted to continue.

*   *   *

The emotive connotations of the term 'positive discrimination' tend to obscure the arguments which the Swann Report fails to consider, arguments that have been accepted in the United States and made effective in the affirmative action legislation that has been in operation for some twenty years. There the avowals of good intention in respect of the appointment of ethnic minority and women applicants failed to be translated into action until legal obligation made it necessary for all educational and other institutions to practise a range of policies which clearly demonstrated and recorded their attempts to gain a representative balance of employees. From both theoretical and practical perspectives the many and varied policies of affirmative action appear to be indistinguishable from those of positive discrimination, yet terminology in such a sensitive area is regarded as being of great importance. The term 'positive discrimination' is considered by many to be misleading and offensive for 'discrimination' *per se* implies a negation of the principles that underlie the legislation, principles that are inextricable from considerations of justice.

Whilst the case for positive discrimination (or affirmative action) cannot be conclusive (for nothing approaching a logical proof is possible) and its acceptability cannot be dependent upon a valid theory of justice (for all existing theories, including those of Rawls (1972) and Walzer (1983) which support it, are critically flawed),[1] there are a number of arguments in its favour that should be carefully considered. They point the way to policies that are capable of rectifying injustice in the areas of staff appointments and promotion with which the Swann Report is concerned.

In our society there is a widely accepted liberal commitment to an egalitarian morality which maintains that people should be treated equally. Provided that is so, it is the individual's own commitment, ingenuity and industry which will result in success, or, if those qualities are absent, in failure (in which case there is no reason for complaint, for the same opportunity was provided). The belief seems to stem from Aristotle's assertion 'that persons who are equal should have assigned to them equal things' and that a rule is unjust 'when either equals have and are awarded unequal shares or unequals equal shares'. It seems clear that the concern is with justice as egalitarianism in a descriptive sense, and not with a normative concept. But elsewhere he uses the two concepts co-extensively: 'Now if the unjust is unequal, the just must be equal'. The distributive rule of justice that Aristotle advances is not unproblematic, for if equals are to be treated equally and unequals unequally in proportion to their relevant differences, there are philosophical questions to be asked about the concepts of equality and relevance that have strong practical ramifications.

From a moral point of view, however, it seems indefensible to claim that race, sex or ethnicity constitute 'relevant' differences on grounds of which appointment or promotion should be refused. Swann rightly affirms the belief that there should be no diminution in standards, yet if applicants are equal in such relevant respects as qualifications and experience, there is no prima facie case for treating them unequally. However, the report states unequivocally that ethnic minority applicants are *not* treated equally, are the victims of (negative) racial discrimination and, in as far as the statement accords with the findings of many other reports on employment and other areas of vital concern, it seems totally inadequate to advocate merely that statistics should be compiled and that 'greater efforts' should be made to remove racist obstacles. Given the fact that the principal obstacle *is* racial prejudice to which none with the power to appoint or promote would admit (or, at least, not openly), stronger remedial action would seem to be necessary.

Experience in the United States shows that previous and existing inequality of opportunity is only rectified when an applicant's race, sex or ethnic origin are regarded as relevant criteria for appointment and promotion, in the interests of securing a more equitable state of affairs. That is not to say, however, that rigid quotas must be enforced, (for then such factors as ethnic origins would be of paramount importance as a criterion for selection, and a likely, if not necessary, consequence *could* be a dimution in standards) but that once the agreed qualifications for employment or promotion are met, race, sex or ethnic origin should be relevant criteria in order to reduce an existing unjust imbalance. A failure of the Swann Report is not that it rejected rigid quotas, but that it failed to consider more sophisticated, enforceable affirmative action policies designed to ensure fairer advertising, interviewing and selection procedures — and the systematic and comprehensive gathering and *use* of statistics to make employers accountable for serious and persistent failure to eliminate racist and sexist practices. The purpose of such policies is to help create a more just state of affairs — a more just society — by virtue of being an effective means of ensuring progress towards a more equitable balance (rather than attempting to effect an immediate transformation), and consequently then can be said to be justified by the *ideal argument* for affirmative action.

It is also possible to defend such policies on the *utilitarian* grounds (attempting to secure the greater happiness of the greatest number of people) that the benefit to society is far greater than the loss entailed, and that no other policies will yield the same gain: in mitigating racism and sexism, they benefit communities and society as a whole. Some of their purpose is to help eradicate self-perpetuating patterns, secure greater equality of opportunity, and operate as a means of gaining greater individual and community happiness. While it is true that philosophers like Bentham and Mill did not succeed in developing a satisfactory, complete system of ethics in utilitarianism (it appears, for example, to vindicate any kind of immoral act provided that it secures the greatest happiness of the greatest number of people), that does not mean that utilitarian arguments do not and should not carry weight. Lord Scarman, one of the most respected and ardent advocates of positive discrimination, has repeatedly advanced an argument that can be given a strictly utilitarian interpretation: it is not that the introduction of positive discrimination will necessarily increase the sum of happiness, but *failure* to introduce such discrimination, in threatening the very stability of our society, will inevitably reduce it. It appears that a similar belief (some may call it political expediency) held sway in the United States when the widespread and very determined civil rights protest of the late 1950s and early 1960s seemed to vanish with the successful, if belated, introduction of civil rights and affirmative action legislation.

The preceding arguments do not depend upon the rectification of previous injustice for their persuasiveness (they are 'forward' and not 'backward' looking); similarly, it is beyond doubt, as the Swann Report states, that in the areas of appointment and promotion injustice *does* exist and consequently affirmative action can gain support by invoking the notions of *compensatory* and *distributive* justice to counter present disadvantage. *De jure* barriers affecting the participation of women, blacks and other minorities in the public world, including educational appointments, have been removed, yet the institutions and ideology that created those barriers persist (which is why it is insufficient merely to recommend their removal). White males continue to occupy a disproportionate percentage of senior positions in the realm of education as elsewhere, have had the benefit of white, male role-models (unlike their female and/or black rivals) and have not had to suffer from the racial discrimination which has such an adverse effect upon the career prospects of ethnic minorities of both sexes.

From the perspective of distributive justice, too, the widespread practice of negative discrimination reinforces the case for affirmative action policies if the benefits and burdens of the market in education — as elsewhere — are to be equally distributed. The relevant consideration is existing injustice to women and ethnic minorities, and the objective to neutralize its effect. The objector from an non-disadvantaged group might claim a denial of equality of opportunity, yet to invoke the latter is to claim violation of an existing equality that manifestly does not exist. The market in education, as elsewhere, should function neutrally: in so far as there is protection of the objector's right to have an application considered with as much care and consideration as those of others, he or she is not being treated unjustly.

*   *   *

I have argued that the Swann Report is seriously at fault in failing to examine these arguments — and in failing to recommend policies that are capable of delivering some of the very changes that it considers to be desirable. These arguments require development in greater detail if they are fully to justify radical changes in current educational policy.

Some of the changes find their justification in the concept of justice *as* equality which entails *effective* equality of opportunity (as distinct from equality of outcome) and should include:

1. The obligatory gathering and use of publicly available statistics on employees' race, ethnic origin and sex, with the objective of achieving a fairer balance.

2. The appointment of affirmative action officers who would be responsible for compiling statistics and ensuring that proper advertising, interviewing and appointment procedures are implemented.

3. The drafting and enactment of law to make employers accountable for serious failure to rectify malpractice.

It is not possible to deal with more than a few aspects of affirmative action in so short a space, but given the perceived importance and urgency of the issues that led to the setting up of the Swann Committee, the detail and comprehensiveness of its research, and the report's authoritative status as a guide for future practice, the failure seems incredible. The reasons are a matter for speculation, but the *fact* of the omission has ensured that a vital area of justice has not been brought to Parliament's attention and will not be publicly debated for the forseeable future. It was an opportunity missed, and one that we may have cause to regret.

Note

1.   It is not possible to substantiate this judgement here; I am examining the arguments of Rawls (1972) and Walzer (1983) in my PhD research on positive discrimination.

References

Ackerman, B. (1980), *Social Justice in the Liberal State*. New Haven and London: Yale University Press.

Aristotle, *Nicomachean Ethics* [113a, 1131a]

_____ *Politics* [1282b]

Aspin, D.N. (1983), 'Church schools, religious education and the multi-ethnic community', *Journal of Philosophy of Education*, Vol.17, No.2, pp.229-40.

Bailey, C. (1984), *Beyond the Present and the Particular: a theory of liberal education*. London: Routledge and Kegan Paul.

Callan, E. (1985), 'McLaughlin on parental rights', *Journal of Philosophy of Education*, Vol.19, No.1, pp.111-18.

Craft, M. (ed.) (1984), *Education and Cultural Pluralism*. Basingstoke: Falmer Press.

Crittenden, B. (1982), *Cultural Pluralism and Common Curriculum*. Melbourne: Melbourne University Press.

Dahrendorf, R. (1982), *On Britain*. London: BBC Publications.

Davey, A. (1975), Racial awareness in children and teacher education', *Education for Teaching*, No.97, Summer.

Dummett, A. (1986), 'Race, culture and moral education', *Journal of Moral Education*, Vol.15, No.1, pp.10-15.

Dunlop, F. (1986), 'The education of the emotions and the promotion of autonomy: are they really compatible?' *British Journal of Educational Studies*, Vol.XXXIV, No.2, pp.152-60.

Dworkin, R. (1977), *Taking Rights Seriously*. London: Duckworth.

Erikson, E. (1968), *Identity: youth and crisis*. London: Faber and Faber.

Evans, G. (1981), 'Semantic theory and tacit knowledge', in S.H. Holtzman and C.M. Leich (eds.), *Wittgenstein: to follow a rule*. London: Routledge and Kegan Paul.

Fielding, M. (1985), 'Celebration — valuing what we do', in R. Blatchford (ed.), *Managing the Secondary School*. London: Bell and Hyman.

Frey, R. (ed.) (1985), *Utility and Rights*. Oxford: Blackwell.

Fromm, E. (1942), *The Fear of Freedom*. London: Routledge and Kegan Paul.

Gadamer, H.G. (1981), *Truth and Method*. London: Sheed and Ward.
_____ (1983), *Reason in the Age of Science*. London and Cambridge, Mass.: MIT Press.
Gewirth, A. (1977), *Reason and Morality*. Chicago: Chicago University Press.
_____ (1984), 'the epistemology of human rights', in Paul, Miller and Paul (eds.)
Godfrey, R. (1984), 'John White and the imposition of autonomy', *Journal of Philosophy of Education*, Vol.18, No.1, pp.115-18.
Gray, J. (1984), 'Indirect utility and fundamental rights' in Paul, Miller and Paul (eds.)
Gumpertz, J.J., Jupp, T.C. and Roberts, C. (1979), *Crosstalk: a study of cross-cultural communication*. London: National Centre for Industrial Language Training.
Gundara, J. et al. (1984), *Race, Education and Research: Rampton, Swann and after*, Working Paper 3. London: Centre for Multicultural Education, Institute of Education, University of London.
Gundara, J., Jones, C. and Kimberley, K. (1986), *Racism, Diversity and Education*. Sevenoaks: Hodder and Stoughton.
Habermas, J. (1976), *Legitimation Crisis*. London: Heinemann Educational.
Haldane, J. (1986) 'Religious education in a pluralist society: a philosophical examination', *British Journal of Educational Studies*, Vol.XXXIV, No.2, pp.161-81.
Halstead, J.M. (1986), *The Case for Muslim Voluntary-aided Schools: some philosophical reflections*. Cambridge: Islamic Academy.
Haydon, G. (1977, 'The "right to education" and compulsory schooling', *Educational Philosophy and Theory*, Vol.9, No.1.
_____ (1979), 'Political theory and the child: problems of the individualist tradition', *Political Studies*, Vol.27, No.3.
_____ (1986), 'Collective moral philosophy and education for pluralism', *Journal of Philosophy of Education*, Vol.20, No.1, pp.97-106.
Hirst, P.H. (1981), 'Education, catechesis and the church school', *British Journal of Religious Education*, Vol.3, No.3, Spring, pp.85-93, 101.
_____ (1985), 'Education and diversity of belief', in M.C. Felderhof (ed.), *Religious Education in a Pluralistic Society*. Sevenoaks: Hodder and Stoughton.
Hirst, P.Q. (1986), *Law, Democracy and Socialism*. London: Allen and Unwin.
Islamic Academy (1985), *Swann Committee Report: an evaluation from the Muslim point of view*. An agreed statement. Cambridge: Islamic Academy.
Jones, M. (1985), 'Education and racism', *Journal of Philosophy of Education*, Vol.19, No.2, pp.225-30.
_____ (1986), 'The Swann Report on "Education for All" : a critique', *Journal of Philosophy of Education*, Vol.20, No.1, pp.107-12.
Kenny, A. (1986), *A Path from Rome*. Oxford: Oxford University Press.

Khan, V.S. (1985), *Language Education for All? Chapter 7 of the Swann Report*, Working Paper 6. London: Centre for Multicultural Education, Institute of Education, University of London.

Lane, R.E. (1982), 'Government and self-esteem', *Political Theory*, Vol. 11, No.1, February.

Linguistic Minorities Project (1983), *Linguistic Minorities in England*. London: Institute of Education, University of London.

Lloyd, D.I. (1980), 'The rational curriculum: a critique', *Journal of Curriculum Studies*, Vol.12, No.4, pp.331-42.

Lukes, S. (1973), *Individualism*. Oxford: Blackwell.

MacIntyre, A. (1981), *After Virtue*. London: Duckworth.

Mackie, J.L. (1975), 'Rights, utility and universalization', in Frey (ed.).

―――― (1977), *Ethics: inventing right and wrong*. Harmondsworth: Penguin.

McLaughlin, T.H. (1984), 'Parental rights and the religious upbringing of children', *Journal of Philosophy of Education*, Vol.18, No.1, pp.75-83.

―――― (1985), 'Religion, upbringing and liberal values: a rejoinder to Eamonn Callan', *Journal of Philosophy of Education*, Vol.19, No.1, pp.119-27.

Mascaro, J. (1977), 'Introduction', *The Upanishads*. Harmondsworth: Penguin.

Milner, D. (1983), *Children and Race Ten Years On*. London: Ward Lock Educational.

Nielsen, K. (1985), *Equality and Liberty: a defence of radical egalitarianism*. Totowa: Rowman and Allanheld.

Nozick, R. (1974), *Anarchy, State and Utopia*. Oxford: Blackwell.

Parvez, G.A. (1968), *Islam: a challenge to religion*. Lahore, Pakistan: Gulberg.

Pateman, C. (1979), *The Problem of Political Obligation*. Chichester: Wiley.

Paul, E., Miller, F. and Paul, J. (eds.) (1984), *Human Rights*. Oxford: Blackwell.

Rampton Report (1981), *West Indian Children in Our Schools*. Interim Report of the Committee of Inquiry into the Education of Children from Ethnic Minority Groups, Cmnd.8273. London: HMSO.

Rawls, J. (1972), *A Theory of Justice*. Oxford: Oxford University Press.

―――― (1985), 'Justice as fairness: political not metaphysical', *Philosophy and Public Affairs*, Vol.14, Summer.

Sachs, D. (1981), 'How to distinguish self-respect from self-esteem', *Philosophy and Public Affairs*, Vol.10, Fall.

Sandel, M. (1982), *Liberalism and the Limits of Justice*. Cambridge: Cambridge University Press.

Scanlon, T. (1982), 'Contractualism and utilitarianism' in A. Sen and B. Williams (eds.), *Utilitarianism and Beyond*. Cambridge: Cambridge University Press.

Scheffler, S. (1982), *The Rejection of Consequentialism*. Oxford: Oxford University Press.

Scruton, R., Ellis-Jones, A. and O'Keefe, D. (1985), *Education and Indoctrination: an attempt at definition and a review of social and political implications*. Harrow:

Education Research Centre.

Singer, M. (1985), 'Moral issues and social problems', *Philosophy*, Vol.60.

Singer, P. (1973), *Democracy and Disobedience*. Oxford: Oxford University Press.

Smith, R. (1985), *Freedom and Discipline*. London: Allen and Unwin.

Stone, M. (1981), *The Education of the Black Child in Britain: the myth of multiracial education*. London: Fontana.

Strawson, P.F. (1977), *Individuals*. London: Methuen University Paperbacks.

Swann Report (1985), *Education for All: Report of the Committee of Inquiry into the Education of Children from Ethnic Minority Groups*, Cmnd. 9453. London: HMSO.

Taylor, C. (1985), *Philosophical Papers* Vols.1 and 2. Cambridge: Cambridge University Press.

Taylor, G. (1985), *Pride, Shame and Guilt*. Oxford: Clarendon Press.

Taylor, M.J. (1986), '"Education for All": some ethical dimensions of the Swann Report', *Journal of Moral Education*, Vol.15, No.1, pp.68-80.

Thiessen, E.J. (1986), 'Educational pluralism and tolerance', paper presented to the Cambridge branch of the Philosophy of Education Society of Great Britain, February.

Thompson, J. and Held, D. (1982), *Habermas: critical debates*. London: Macmillan.

Troyna, B. and Williams, J. (1986), *Racism, Education and the State*. London: Croom Helm.

Tucker, R.C. (ed.) (1972), *The Marx-Engels Reader*. New York: Norton.

Waldron, J. (ed.) (1984), *Theories of Rights*. Oxford: Oxford University Press.

Walsh, P.D. (1983), 'The church secondary school and its curriculum', in P. O'Leary (ed.), *Religious Education and Young Adults*. Slough: St Paul Publications.

Walzer, M. (1983), *Spheres of Justice*. Oxford: Martin Robertson.

Ward, K. (1983), 'Is autonomy an educational ideal?' *Educational Analysis*, Vol.5, No.1, pp.47-55.

White, J. (1984a), 'A reply to Raymond Godfrey', *Journal of Philosophy of Education*, Vol.18, No.1, pp.119-21.

_____ (1984b), 'The education of the emotions', *Journal of Philosophy of Education*, Vol.18, No.2, pp.233-44.

White, J. and White, P. (1986), 'Education, liberalism and human good', in D.E. Cooper (ed.), *Education, Values and Mind: essays for R.S. Peters*. London: Routledge and Kegan Paul.

Wiener, M. (1981), *English Culture and the Decline of the Industrial Spirit, 1850-1980*. Cambridge: Cambridge University Press.

Williams, B. (1985), *Ethics and the Limits of Philosophy*. London: Fontana.